At Issue

Voter Fraud

Other Books in the At Issue Series:

At Issue

Voter Fraud

Sarah Armstrong, Book Editor

GREENHAVEN PRESS
A part of Gale, Cengage Learning

GALE
CENGAGE Learning·

Farmington Hills, Mich • San Francisco • New York • Waterville, Maine
Meriden, Conn • Mason, Ohio • Chicago

GALE
CENGAGE Learning·

Judy Galens, *Manager, Frontlist Acquisitions*

© 2016 Greenhaven Press, a part of Gale, Cengage Learning.

Gale and Greenhaven Press are registered trademarks used herein under license.

For more information, contact:
Greenhaven Press
27500 Drake Rd.
Farmington Hills, MI 48331-3535
Or you can visit our Internet site at gale.cengage.com

Articles in Greenhaven Press anthologies are often edited for length to meet page require-ments. In addition, original titles of these works are changed to clearly present the main thesis and to explicitly indicate the author's opinion. Every effort is made to ensure that Greenhaven Press accurately reflects the original intent of the authors. Every effort has been made to trace the owners of copyrighted material.

Cover image © Images.com/Corbis.

LIBRARY OF CONGRESS CATALOGING-IN-PUBLICATION DATA

Names: Armstrong, Sarah, 1979- editor.
Title: Voter fraud / Sarah Armstrong, book editor.
Description: Farmington Hills, Mich : Greenhaven Press, a part of Gale, Cengage Learning, [2016] | Series: At issue | Includes bibliographical references and index.
Identifiers: LCCN 2015030376 | ISBN 9780737773705 (hardcover) | ISBN 9780737773712 (pbk.)
Subjects: LCSH: Elections--Corrupt practices--United States. | Political corruption--United States. | United States--Politics and government.
Classification: LCC JK1994 .V68 2016 | DDC 324.6/60973--dc23
LC record available at http://lccn.loc.gov/2015030376

Printed in Mexico
1 2 3 4 5 6 7 20 19 18 17 16

Contents

Introduction

Eric Kennie, a US citizen and lifelong Texan, has always taken his right to vote as a serious responsibility. He proudly voted for Barack Obama in 2008, participated in the midterm elections in 2010, and voted for Obama again in 2012. "Ever since he turned 18 he has made a point of voting in general elections, having been brought up by his African American parents to think that it is important, part of what he calls 'doing the right thing.'"[1] Yet he, along with more than half a million other Texans, were turned away from the voting polls in November 2014 under the state's new voter ID law— Senate Bill 14 (SB14)—which denies voting privileges to those who fail to produce proper photo identification. When asked how he felt about being denied his constitutional right to vote, Kennie said, "It makes me hurt deep down inside, it really do."[2]

Few things in American history have been more contentious than the right to vote, often intersecting with issues of gender, immigration, and race. Susan B. Anthony began the often-violent women's suffrage movement in 1869, but it would take more than half a century before women were granted electoral privileges under the Nineteenth Amendment. Native Americans were banned from voting until 1924, when the Indian Citizenship Act granted them the rights of citizenship. Similarly, Asian Americans, specifically hundreds of thousands of Chinese immigrants, found their citizenship and voting rights suppressed under an anti-immigrant law called the Chinese Exclusion Act, which would not be overturned until 1943. African American men were legally granted the freedom

---

1. Ed Pilkington, "'Born and Raised' Texans Forced to Prove Identities Under New Voter ID Law," *Guardian*, October 27, 2014. http://www.theguardian.com/us-news/2014/oct/27/texas-vote-id-proof-certificate-minority-law.
2. Ibid.

to vote in 1869, with the passage of the Fifteenth Amendment, but lawmakers and supremacists initiated legislatively creative means to suppress their vote for the next century, employing such practices as grandfather clauses for former slaves, literacy tests, and poll taxes.

One of the issues central to the civil rights movement was the basic constitutional right to a fair and free election for African Americans. On May 17, 1957, before a crowd gathered at the Lincoln Memorial during the March on Washington, Reverend Martin Luther King Jr. said:

> [A]ll types of conniving methods are still being used to prevent Negroes from becoming registered voters. The denial of this sacred right is a tragic betrayal of the highest mandates of our democratic traditions and it is democracy turned upside down. So long as I do not firmly and irrevocably possess the right to vote I do not possess myself. I cannot make up my mind—it is made up for me. I cannot live as a democratic citizen, observing the laws I have helped to enact—I can only submit to the edict of others. So our most urgent request to the president of the United States and every member of Congress is to give us the right to vote. Give us the ballot and we will no longer have to worry the federal government about our basic rights.[3]

Nearly eight years after giving that speech, King led over five hundred nonviolent protestors on a five-day march from Selma, Alabama, to the capitol building in Montgomery to campaign for African American voting rights. On March 7, 1965, the march gained national attention when news cameras broadcasted footage of Alabama state troopers violently attacking the peaceful demonstrators. The event became known as "Bloody Sunday." At the close of the march, King said, "Our whole campaign in Alabama has been centered around the

---

3. Martin Luther King Jr., "Give Us the Ballot, We Will Transform the South," speech given on May 17, 1957, Lincoln Memorial, Washington, DC. http://www.pbs.org/pov /pov2008/election/wvote/king.html.

right to vote. In focusing the attention of the nation and the world today on the flagrant denial of the right to vote, we are exposing the very origin, the root cause, of racial segregation in the Southland."[4]

While the Selma march began violently it ended in victory, paving the way for the Voting Rights Act of 1965, which President Lyndon Johnson signed into law on August 6, 1965, five months after "Bloody Sunday."

Yet there are many who claim that, even today, the voting rights of African Americans and minorities continue to be challenged by lawmakers—now under the guise of stringent voter ID laws like SB14 in Texas, implemented to prevent electoral fraud. Defendants of the bill, such as Texas senator John Cornyn, insist that "the law is reasonable, and it is popular. Protecting the integrity of the voting process is something that benefits everyone. The Supreme Court has held that voter ID laws are constitutional."[5] Opponents of the law, such as Supreme Court Justice Ruth Bader Ginsburg, in a scathing dissenting opinion, claimed that the intent of the law is not only "purposefully discriminatory," but that "Senate Bill 14 may prevent more than 600,000 registered Texas voters (about 4.5% of all registered voters) from voting in person for lack of compliant identification. . . . A sharply disproportionate percentage of those voters are African-American or Hispanic."[6] On October 9, 2014, less than two years after the bill was initially passed into law, a US district judge from the Fifth Circuit Court in Corpus Christi, Texas, swiftly struck down SB 14 on the grounds that the bill "creates a substantial burden on

4. Martin Luther King Jr., "Address at the Conclusion of the Selma to Montgomery March," March 25, 1965. http://kingencyclopedia.stanford.edu/encyclopedia/documentsentry/doc_address_at_the_conclusion_of_selma_march.

5. John Cornyn, "Voter ID Protects Voter Equality," *Austin American-Statesman*, August 8, 2013. http://www.statesman.com/news/news/opinion/cornyn-voter-id-protects-voter-equality/nZHXB.

6. Ruth Bader Ginsburg, dissenting opinion in *Veasey et al. v. Perry*, 574 U.S., October 18, 2014. http://www.supremecourt.gov/opinions/14pdf/14a393_08m1.pdf.

the fundamental right to vote, has a discriminatory effect and purpose, and constitutes a poll tax."[7]

The issue of whether voter ID laws help to deter electoral fraud—or if, in fact, they simply constitute a new form of racism—remains a hotly contested issue in American politics. *At Issue: Voter Fraud* examines both sides of the debate as well as probes other issues relating to electoral fraud, such as gerrymandering, felon re-enfranchisement, and noncitizen voting.

7. *Veasey et al. v. Perry et al.*, Civil Action No. 13-CV-00193 (TXSD 2014). http://electionlawblog.org/wp-content/uploads/20141009-TXID-Opinion.pdf.

Broad Support for Photo ID Voting Requirements

Pew Research Center

Pew Research Center is a nonprofit, nonpartisan research organization dedicated to informing the public about current trends in US politics, social sciences, demographics, and public opinion.

The overwhelming majority of Americans support the requirement to show photo identification in order to place a vote, according to a September 2012 survey conducted by Pew Research Center for the People & the Press. While there are partisan differences on the issue, most Americans favor the requirement regardless of their political standing. Most are also aware whether or not photo identification is required by law to vote in their state.

Proposals to require voters to show photo identification before being allowed to vote draw overwhelming support. By 77% to 20%, voters favor a requirement that those voting be required to show photo ID. Opinion about this is little changed from six years ago, when 80% of voters supported voter photo ID requirements.

Several states have enacted strict photo ID voting requirements, but there have been court challenges to many of these laws. Last week, a Pennsylvania judge blocked enforcement of that state's voter ID law.

In a national survey of 1,263 registered voters, conducted Sept. 12–16 by the Pew Research Center for the People & the Press, nearly all (98%) say they are confident that they have the identification they will need at the polls on Nov. 6.

There are partisan differences in views of photo ID requirements for voters, though majorities of Republicans, Democrats, and independents favor such requirements. Fully 95% of Republican voters say a photo ID should be required to vote, as do 83% of independents. By comparison, 61% of Democrats who say photo identification should be required; 34% say it should not. Liberal Democrats are about equally divided on this question (46% should be required, 48% should not).

Support for photo identification laws is somewhat higher among voters in states with some voter identification requirements . . . than among those in states without laws requiring voters to show identification at the polls.

Most Voters in States with Photo ID Laws Know About Requirements

Just four states (Georgia, Indiana, Kansas and Tennessee) have strict photo identification requirements in effect for the 2012 election, in which voters must show official photo identification to vote. About nine-in-ten voters (92%) in these states know that their state requires photo identification.

Laws vary in other states, but for the most part, voters are aware of the voting requirements in their state. About three-quarters (77%) of voters in states where photo ID requirements are less stringent know that a photo ID is required. And 67% of those in states with requirements for identification (though not necessarily photo identification) say photo identification is required.

Many states have no voter identification requirements, and 48% of voters in these states correctly say that their state does not require photo identification, although 38% say that photo identification is required to vote in their state.

Support for photo identification laws is somewhat higher among voters in states with some voter identification requirements (83%) than among those in states without laws requiring voters to show identification at the polls (70%).

Voter Fraud Is Real but It Can Be Stopped

The Heritage Foundation

The Heritage Foundation is a conservative think tank that conducts research and promotes public policies in support of its core principles of free enterprise, limited government, strong national security, and traditional American values.

The US Constitution guarantees that free and fair elections are the basic right of every American. Voter fraud, however, is a serious concern and a threat to the integrity of the electoral process. There are many types of voter fraud including impersonation at the polls, buying votes, duplicate voting, and more. Voter ID laws can help prevent voter fraud and are supported by the majority of Americans.

Preserving the great experiment that is the American Republic is dependent upon free and fair elections. Whether you are selecting a city councilor or the President, every American must be able to trust the process and the result, or the democratic system breaks down. Election integrity is an essential part of free and fair elections. As an eligible citizen, you must be guaranteed the right to vote—and it must be guaranteed that your vote is not stolen or diluted by thieves and fraudsters. . . .

But why would someone steal your vote? Elections are avenues to political power and prestige. So long as they are, there will be those who would rather steal a vote than leave their ambitions vulnerable to your opinions. Chicago saw this firsthand in 1982, when 100,000 fraudulent ballots were cast in a massive effort to swing an election. Some who oppose measures intended to prevent election fraud claim there is not enough fraud to justify such election integrity efforts, but as the National Commission on Federal Election Reform said, the problem "is not the magnitude of voter fraud. In close or disputed elections, and there are many, a small amount of fraud could make the margin of difference."

There are many different forms of voter and election fraud that can be used to steal votes or change the outcome of an election.

How Long Has Voter Fraud Been a Problem?

The U.S. Supreme Court has said that "flagrant examples" of voter fraud "have been documented throughout this Nation's history by respected historians and journalists." The instances of such fraud uncovered over the years "demonstrate that not only is the risk of voter fraud real but that it could affect the outcome of a close election."

Coordinated attempts to commandeer election results are not a modern invention. Instances have been documented in the United States dating as far back as the early 19th century. New York City's infamous political organization, Tammany Hall, was synonymous with election fraud—in one election in 1844 there were 55,000 votes recorded even though there were only 41,000 eligible voters. Those early traditions of voter fraud have continued and grown ever more inventive. In 1984, a state grand jury report released in Kings County, New York detailed a 14-year-long successful voter fraud conspiracy in Brooklyn that resulted in thousands of fraudulent votes being cast in New York legislative and congressional elections through impersonation fraud and false registrations.

Types of Voter Fraud

There are many different forms of voter and election fraud that can be used to steal votes or change the outcome of an election. These include:

- Impersonation Fraud at the Polls—Voting in the names of other legitimate voters and voters who have died, moved away, or lost their right to vote because they are felons, but remain registered.

- False Registrations—Voting under fraudulent voter registrations that either use a phony name and a real or fake address or claim residence in a particular jurisdiction where the registered voter does not actually live and is not entitled to vote.

- Duplicate Voting—Registering in multiple locations and voting in the same election in more than one jurisdiction or state.

- Fraudulent Use of Absentee Ballots—Requesting and voting with absentee ballots without the knowledge of the actual voter; or obtaining the absentee ballot from a voter and either filling it in directly and forging the voter's signature or illegally telling the voter who to vote for on the ballot.

- Buying Votes—Paying voters to cast either an in-person or absentee ballot for a particular candidate.

- Illegal "Assistance" at the Polls—Forcing or intimidating voters—particularly the elderly, disabled, illiterate, and those for whom English is a second language—to vote for particular candidates while supposedly providing them with "assistance."

- Ineligible Voting—Illegal registration and voting by individuals who are not U.S. citizens, or are convicted felons, and therefore are not eligible to vote.

- Altering the Vote Count—Changing the actual vote count either in a precinct or at the central location where votes are counted.

- Ballot Petition Fraud—Forging the signatures of registered voters on the ballot petitions that must be filed with election officials in some states for a candidate to be listed on the official ballot.

Recommended Ways to Protect Your Vote

There are several steps that can be taken to improve the integrity of both the voter registration and voting processes. These procedures will not stop all forms of fraud practiced by vote thieves, but when implemented and enforced in combination, they can be a powerful weapon to deter and prevent many types of voter fraud—and they do not prevent eligible citizens from voting.

Several states ... have implemented voter ID laws in recent years to prevent and detect voter fraud.

Preventing fraud in the first place is much easier than trying to detect, investigate, and prosecute it after it occurs. Without proper procedures in place, detecting voter fraud is an extremely difficult undertaking. Moreover, prosecutors faced with burgeoning caseloads often give a very low priority to prosecuting election fraud, especially after the election is over.

Procedures that election officials can and should implement to secure your vote include:

- Photographic, Government-issued Identification to Vote—Photo IDs should be required for both in-person

17

voting and absentee balloting. With absentee ballots, voters should be required to provide either a photocopy of the ID when they mail in the absentee ballot or the identification number of their state-issued driver's license or photo ID card. For the small percentage of individuals who do not already have an ID, states should issue free ID cards for voting.

- Proof of Citizenship to Register to Vote—Anyone registering to vote should be required to provide proof of U.S. citizenship such as a birth certificate, naturalization papers, or other documents including those that the federal government requires all employers to check before hiring a new employee.

- Jury Forms and Department of Homeland Security Databases—All state and federal courts should be required to notify local election officials when individuals summoned for jury duty from voter registration rolls are excused because they are not U.S. citizens. All state voter registration databases should run frequent comparisons with noncitizen databases maintained by the Department of Homeland Security to detect individuals who have registered to vote but who are not citizens.

- Interstate Voter Registration Crosscheck Program—The State of Kansas initiated a program to compare state voter registration rolls to detect individuals who are registered in more than one state and may have voted unlawfully in the same election in different states. All states should participate in this program to increase the accuracy of voter registration information and detect possible fraud.

- Accuracy Checks of Voter Registration Information— All states should verify the accuracy of their voter registration information by comparing it with other information databases such as Department of Motor Vehicle driver's license and Social Security Administration records, as well as tax and other county and state records.

Debunking Myths

Several states, including Alabama, Georgia, Indiana, Kansas, Mississippi, Rhode Island, South Carolina, Tennessee, and Texas, have implemented voter ID laws in recent years to prevent and detect voter fraud.

Studies of past elections support the conclusion that voter ID laws have not reduced the turnout rates of minority voters.

Critics of voter ID laws claim that requiring the presentation of a valid ID can only prevent impersonation fraud at the polling place. Voter ID laws, however, can also prevent the misuse and theft of absentee ballots if identification is required for both forms of voting. Such laws can also prevent individuals from voting under fictitious voter registrations or voting by aliens, whether they are present legally or illegally in the country. In some instances, voter ID laws may prevent double voting by individuals registered in more than one state or locality if the information on their ID does not match their registration information or they try to use an ID from another state to vote.

Perhaps the biggest myth about voter ID laws is that they depress turnout, especially by minority voters. Years of turnout data from states that have photo ID laws show the opposite. Wherever photo ID requirements have been implemented, they have not reduced turnout. In fact, minority turnout has gone up in photo ID states. For example, in 2008, after implementing new voter ID laws, both Georgia and Indiana experienced larger increases in turnout, including of minority voters, in the presidential election than many states without a photo ID requirement. In Georgia, the turnout of both Hispanics and Africans Americans increased dramatically in both the 2008 presidential and 2010 midterm congressional elections when compared to the 2004 presidential and 2006 congressional elections when there was no photo ID requirement in place.

The U.S. Census Bureau conducts a survey of turnout after every federal election and provides a table detailing turnout by race in every state. According to the Census, in the 2012 presidential election, the black turnout rate in Georgia was higher than white turnout even with its voter ID requirement in place. In 2012, in Indiana, which has one of the strictest voter ID laws in the country, black voter turnout was 10 percentage points higher than white voter turnout. In 2012, in Tennessee, which had just implemented its voter ID law, black voter turnout was three percentage points higher than white voter turnout.

Other studies of past elections support the conclusion that voter ID laws have not reduced the turnout rates of minority voters. One such study concluded that "concerns about voter identification laws affecting turnout are much ado about nothing."

Polling shows that requiring ID to vote (as well as requiring proof of citizenship to register) is consistently supported by a majority of Americans no matter their race, ethnicity, socioeconomic status or party affiliation. That is no doubt because they know that they need an ID in their everyday lives to cash a check, buy alcohol or tobacco, purchase cold medicine or get a prescription filled in some states, see their doctor, take the SAT, buy a gun, check into a hotel, get a fishing or hunting license, open a post office box, board an airplane, obtain a marriage license, or get into many government buildings.

3

Voter Fraud Is a Legitimate Threat

James Simpson

James Simpson, a former White House analyst, is an investigative journalist, economist, and businessman. His work has appeared in Washington Times, WorldNetDaily, *and* American Thinker, *among other publications.*

Democrats espouse the theory that voter registration fraud is a myth, but this is deceitful propaganda that serves their own interests. Voter roll programs such as Crosscheck, designed to clean up voter roll databases, have confirmed evidence of voter fraud, including thousands of duplicate registrations, invalid addresses, and deceased voters. Democrats have also created legislation that encourages voter fraud among college students, based on their domicile status. Other initiatives, such as the National Popular Vote Interstate Compact, Universal Voter Registration, and felon re-enfranchisement, further Democrats' duplicitous schemes and threaten the integrity of the American electoral system.

It is difficult to describe the enormity of the crime being committed by the [Barack] Obama administration and their Democratic allies. They flagrantly flout the law, while simultaneously turning it into a weapon against political opponents, use government agencies to target innocent Americans, attempt to create legal voters through amnesty, and undermine voter integrity measures to facilitate vote fraud, while denying it even exists. In short, they are corrupting the entire process.

Thus, it is fitting to begin this report by recounting a story of deliberate, blatant official voter fraud. This April 17 [2014], the Illinois House Executive Committee voted to authorize $100 million to construct President Obama's future presidential library and museum in Chicago. AP [Associated Press] reported that the Committee voted "unanimously," 9-0 to support the plan. The report was false. Only four of the 11 Committee members were in attendance—all Democrats. They did not even have a quorum. Furthermore, this was supposed to be a "subject matter only" hearing, i.e., entailing no votes. No matter; the legislators simply made up the results—even counting absent Republicans as "yes" votes. Republican State Representative Ed Sullivan observed, "In this case they didn't even care to change the rules; they just flat out broke them."

The [National Voter Registration Act] was authored by socialists Richard Cloward and Frances Fox Piven, and many believe it was deliberately constructed to pave the way for ACORN-style massive registration fraud.

Motor Voter

The National Voter Registration Act (NVRA), also known as "motor voter," promotes easy voter registration at motor vehicle, welfare and other state and local government offices. Voters can apply in person or by mail, and, until a recent court ruling, the federal application required no proof of citizenship. The NVRA also dictates voter roll maintenance, but it is a confusing procedure that can take over two election cycles. States have also frequently been lackadaisical about taking advantage of the methods afforded by the law. Some election boards actually have to be sued to clean up their voter rolls.

As a result, nationwide, voter rolls are a shambles. According to a Pew report, approximately 24 million voter registrations nationally are either invalid or inaccurate, including about 1.8 million deceased individuals and 2.75 million multistate duplicates.

The NVRA was authored by socialists Richard Cloward and Frances Fox Piven, and many believe it was deliberately constructed to pave the way for ACORN-style massive registration fraud. The pair is notorious for the Cloward/Piven Crisis Strategy—a plan to overwhelm government with demands for welfare spending, thereby leading to systemic crisis. Cloward and Piven helped launch ACORN to advance their strategy.

They also had other intentions for those burgeoning welfare rolls. "If organizers can deliver millions of dollars in cash benefits to the ghetto masses," they wrote, "it seems reasonable to expect that the masses will deliver their loyalties to their benefactors." Cloward and Piven developed the Motor Voter idea to simplify voter registration for this demographic. In 1993, it became law. Successive NRVA lawsuits have forced state agencies to become *de facto* taxpayer-funded voter registration drives.

Through its criminal activities, massive voter registration fraud and numerous convictions, ACORN made voter fraud national news. Prodded, and in some cases sued by activists, state legislatures began cleaning voter rolls and enacting ballot integrity measures like photo voter ID.

Voter Suppression

Democrats responded by executing a nationwide propaganda campaign of contrived outrage to deliver one relentless message: widespread voter fraud is a myth created by racist Republicans to justify voter ID and other laws that suppress the minority vote. MSNBC even called it a war on voting.

This President [Barack Obama] has proven over and over, however, that Democrats lie, and the Obama administration has institutionalized the practice. As Robert Popper writes in *The Wall Street Journal*:

> In an April 11 speech to Al Sharpton's National Action Network, President Obama recited statistics purporting to show that voter fraud was extremely rare. The "real voter fraud," he said, "is people who try to deny our rights by making bogus arguments about voter fraud."

Popper responds, "These arguments themselves are bogus."

Having rationalized the moral high ground with their "voter suppression" charge—Democrats go on the warpath. In recent years this has involved lawsuits, organized slander and a nationwide campaign to resist election reform.

And of course he's right. While they deny, obfuscate and attack, Democrats don't even bother to hide their true intentions. In an event that can only be described as *bad optics* for the President, Sharpton's NAN had just hosted a "Welcome Home Party" for serial convicted vote fraudster Melowese Richardson. After serving only eight months of a five year sentence for her crimes, Richardson was celebrated by Sharpton as a conquering hero.

Voter Fraud as Reparations

Democrats' attitude toward voter fraud is the voting version of reparations for slavery. Some Democrats have even said that because minorities and the poor have little influence, "extraordinary measures (for example, stretching the absentee ballot or registration rules) are required to compensate." Democrat election officials do this all the time, and a form of it has actually become official Justice Department policy in its effort to boost Hispanic representation.

Hispanic voters in Port Chester, New York were allowed to use something called "cumulative voting" in an election for village trustees. There were six trustee seats and Hispanics were allowed to cast six votes in any way they chose, for example, casting one vote for each of six candidates or all six for one candidate. Cumulative voting has also been used to elect a school board in Amarillo, Texas, the county commission in Chilton County, Alabama, and the city council in Peoria, Illinois.

Having rationalized the moral high ground with their *"voter suppression"* charge—Democrats go on the warpath. In recent years this has involved lawsuits, organized slander and a nationwide campaign to resist election reform. Under the Obama presidency, it has also included using federal agencies to attack private citizens and organizations. . . .

Crosscheck Program

In 2005, the Kansas, Iowa, Nebraska and Missouri Secretaries of State agreed to initiate a program called "Crosscheck." Participating states provide voter data for comparison with voter rolls in other states. One can compare first name, last and date of birth, vote history, and when states provide it, the last four digits of the voter's Social Security number. This can uncover duplicate registrations, and, potentially, voter fraud. Starting with only those four states, the Crosscheck program has now grown to 28.

The numbers of potential duplicate registrations are astronomical, about 3.5 million for the participating 28 states, but the data must be evaluated with caution. Kansas Secretary of State Kris Kobach states that surprisingly, there are many Americans with an identical first name, last name and date of birth (DOB). Election lawyer J. Christian Adams also warns that voter records are notorious for data entry errors. Still, individual Crosscheck states have found striking results worthy of closer scrutiny. North Carolina's State Board of Elections (SBOE) analyzed Crosscheck data for 2012 and found:

- 765 voters with matching first and last name, DOB and last four digits of SSN registered in NC and another state, *and* voted in both.

- 35,750 voters with the same first and last name and DOB registered in NC and another state *and* voted in both. (This includes data from states that do not provide SSN info.). Approximately one-third (11,560) came from border states.

- 155,692 voters with the same first and last name, DOB and last four digits of SSN registered in NC and another state—and the latest date of registration or voter activity was not in NC.

Vote thieves access the voter database and commit vote fraud using names of inactive voters.

SBOE Director Kim Strach warned against reading too much into the crosscheck numbers yet. The SBOE intends to examine each record individually. Separately, the SBOE also revealed:

- 50,000 new death records not previously provided to SBOE

- 13,416 deceased voters on the rolls in October 2013

- 81 deceased voters that had voter activity after they died

Other groups have explored voter rolls and found numerous problems. The Virginia Voters Alliance worked with Election Integrity Maryland and found 44,000 registration matches. The group also found 31,000 dead voters on the Virginia rolls. The North Carolina Voter Integrity Project handed over 20,000 voters with invalid addresses to the SBOE, and identified 5,167 dual registrations in Florida, of which at least 147 appear to be "either a victim or perpetrator" of voter fraud. In 2013, Kansas found 484 potential double voters through crosscheck. Twenty-one were referred for prosecution.

Double voting is only one explanation for dual votes, however, and perhaps not the main one. Susan Myrick of North Carolina's Civitas Institute, a veteran elections official, has long believed that vote thieves access the voter database and commit vote fraud using names of inactive voters. Vote officials could never prove it before, but now Crosscheck provides a methodology.

Out-of-State Voters

Democrats now openly say "vote where your vote will count," i.e., if you live in a dark red or blue state, your vote is wasted; go vote in a swing state. However, in order to do so legally, one must establish residency in the target swing state. How does one establish residency where one does not actually live, or intend to live for any extended period?

A long time ago, the Left began calculating ways to do this. The most promising demographic was college students. They are reliably liberal, reliably malleable, and move temporarily in large numbers. In 1972, the ACLU's New Hampshire chapter brought a class action suit in US District Court on behalf of an out-of-state Dartmouth college student who was denied the right to vote in NH because he informed authorities he intended to leave NH upon graduation. The judge ruled that out-of-state students could vote in NH, as long as they were "domiciled" in NH.

Black's Law Dictionary defines "Domicile" as "not for a mere special or temporary purpose, but with the present intention of making a permanent home, until some unexpected event shall occur to induce him to adopt some other permanent home." Normally, your domicile is where you live permanently, where you are licensed to drive, where you pay taxes, are called for jury duty, etc. That is usually not a college dorm.

Leftists love [same day registration voting] because it simplifies the task of getting out the vote and makes verification difficult.

One can immediately see the irony in the judge's ruling. For example, how can a student be classified as out-of-state for tuition purposes and yet "domiciled" in-state to vote? What about NH residents who go out-of-state to attend college? New Hampshire still considers them NH residents. This out-of-state condition is called "temporary absence." Why then are out-of-state students attending school in NH not considered to be temporarily absent from their own home state, and thus ineligible to vote in NH?

Today, out-of-state students in all 50 states can vote wherever they attend college. This has created essentially two classes of voter. Laws vary, but in many states students don't have to meet usual residency requirements, like registering a car. Cloistered away on campus, students are largely insulated from state and local politics. They will bear no long-term consequence for the outcomes of those elections, yet their sheer numbers guarantee a heavy influence. For example, residents could be saddled with a tax-and-spend governor because students who will never feel the impact voted for that candidate.

This has been further facilitated by same day registration/voting.

Same Day Registration/Voting

Same day voting allows a person to register to vote, and then vote on the same day. Leftists love it because it simplifies the task of getting out the vote and makes verification difficult. Some states require photo ID and other supporting documentation to prove the registrant's residence, but many do not. Some states check registrations later; many don't bother.

Cloward and Piven wrote an exemption into the NVRA for states that allow same day voter/registration. This is a big incentive to avoid the NVRA's arduous voter registration requirements, and is yet more proof of the law's subversive goals. . . .

Students Recruited to Support Local Political Machines

In April, 2013, the Pasquotank County, North Carolina Board of Elections sustained 57 of 60 voter registration challenges. All voters listed Elizabeth City State University (ECSU) as their residence. None of the sustained challenges were current students. One was not a U.S. citizen. One admitted she lived in California but voted absentee in NC. One lived in Virginia but admitted voting in NC. Another was a recent graduate who registered in Florida and North Carolina on the same day. He made his NC registration online, a violation of state law. However, in 2012, the (then) Democratic SBOE flouted the law and allowed online voting.

[The National Popular Vote Interstate Compact] would bias the election in favor of large population centers—which are usually 80 percent or more Democratic—that could dictate the outcome of presidential elections.

Former Pasquotank County Board of Elections official Betsy Meads asserts that ECSU students are regularly told to register and vote in local elections, even if domiciled elsewhere. ECSU students told Deputy Elections Director Bonnie Godfrey that they were promised perfect grades for voting. Some students said voting was "mandatory." In another case, the ECSU cheerleading squad was ordered to register and vote, despite out-of-town domiciles. When one refused, the cheerleading coach yelled, "Get in there and vote." Almost all did.

Voter ID

Eric Holder's DOJ [Department of Justice] has moved mountains to forestall or prevent legislatures from enacting voter ID, but things have been slowly changing. In 2013 the Supreme Court struck down key parts of the 1965 Voting Rights Act, which required certain states to obtain approval, or preclearance, to change voting laws. As of February 2014, 34 states have voter I.D., but only eight states have strict photo voter ID laws.

National Popular Vote Interstate Compact (NPV)

NPV is an unconstitutional nationwide movement wherein states agree to award all presidential electors to the popular vote winner, regardless of how the state voted. Direct elections become universal when enough state legislatures have joined to make up a majority of the electoral vote (270 of 538). As of April 15, 2014, 10 states plus DC have joined, totaling 165 electoral votes, 61 percent of the 270 needed. Bills have also been passed by one House in Arkansas, Colorado, Connecticut, Delaware, Maine, Michigan, Nevada, New Mexico, North Carolina and Oregon.

NPV would bias the election in favor of large population centers—which are usually 80 percent or more Democratic—that could dictate the outcome of presidential elections. The Electoral College was enshrined in the Constitution to guarantee less populous states influence in federal elections. Political analyst Dick Morris also predicts much more voter fraud if the NPV goes through. Because large cities will be more important, Democrats will pull out all the stops to pad the vote.

Universal Voter Registration

UVR calls for automatically registering voters listed on various state and federal databases. Cloward and Piven's goal has always been UVR. They described NVRA as an intermediate step, but UVR will create even more problems:

1. UVR undermines the Constitution

2. UVR facilitates illegal alien voting

3. State and federal lists create duplicates

4. Duplicates are likely to go uncorrected

Leftists chant the UVR mantra. *Nation Magazine* editor Katrina vanden Heuvel even cited UVR's great success in Russia and Venezuela! However, under our noses the Obama administration has achieved a form of UVR with passage of Obamacare. The law provides for online voter registration. DEMOS has projected that this will register 68 million new voters.

Felon Voting

Eric Holder has added his voice to the chorus of demands to allow for felon voting, another reliable Democratic demographic.

Voter fraud, and the corrupt political infrastructure that facilitates, or at best ignores it, is an existential threat to our American Republic. The only answer is to elect principled conservative leaders willing to recognize and confront this threat.

Voter Fraud in the United States Is Virtually Nonexistent

The Daily Take Team

The Daily Take Team is a group of writers at the nonprofit web-based news outlet Truthout, which provides progressive daily news commentary about underreported issues and original opinion pieces.

Republicans have attempted to pass more than one thousand voter ID bills in the states, but these laws have more to do with limiting Democrats' access to the ballot than preventing voter fraud. Actual occurrences of voter fraud are exceedingly rare— perhaps even nonexistent—and voter ID laws not only suppress American citizens' right to vote but are also a waste of taxpayer money and resources.

The Republicans have finally found voter fraud, and in Ohio no less!

For years, Republicans have been putting laws in place all across America, in an effort to combat what they say is a rampant voter fraud problem.

Since 2001, nearly 1,000 bills that would tighten voting laws have been introduced in 46 states, and since 2011, 24 voting restrictions have gone into effect in 17 states, including battleground states like Florida, Ohio, and Pennsylvania.

The Real Intent of Voter ID Laws

34 States have introduced laws requiring voters to show photo ID since 2011, and in 2008, nearly 2.2 million registered voters did not vote because they didn't have the proper ID required by law.

But don't be fooled by all of these laws, because they have absolutely nothing to do with combatting voter fraud, and have everything to do with keeping typically Democratic voters away from the polls.

This doesn't have anything to do with stopping voter fraud.

According to the Brennan Center for Justice, the top 5 demographic groups that lack a valid photo ID are blacks, Asians, Latinos, and 18-to-24-year-olds.

And, not surprisingly, these are all portions of the population that Democrats typically win, and Republicans typically lose.

So this doesn't have anything to do with stopping voter fraud.

But don't tell that to Republicans in Ohio and across the country, who to this day, are still positive that America is home to rampant cases of voter fraud, that, as Senator John McCain said in 2008, are "destroying the fabric of our democracy."

On Monday [March 11, 2013], the prosecutor's office in Hamilton County, Ohio announced voter fraud charges against three people—including a nun.

According to the prosecutor's office, the nun, Sister Marguerite Kloos, lived with Sister Rose Marie Hewitt until Hewitt's death in October of 2012. Hewitt had requested an absentee ballot for the November election, and the ballot arrived in the mail just days after she died. Kloos allegedly filled it out, forged Hewitt's signature, and mailed it back.

Of course, voter fraud is illegal, and if Sister Kloos did in fact commit voter fraud, she should be held accountable for her actions.

But is finding one person who allegedly committed voter fraud really worth disenfranchising millions of Americans?

Voter Fraud Cases
Are Virtually Nonexistant

Between 2000 and 2010, there were 649 million votes cast in general elections, and only 13 credible cases of voter fraud.

In comparison, during that same period of time, there were 47,000 UFO sightings in the United States, and 441 Americans were killed by lightnings strikes.

Legitimate cases of voter fraud in this country are extraordinarily rare. In fact, you have a better chance of dying from a TV falling on your head than you do of finding a case of voter fraud.

And, states that have introduced voter suppression ID laws are having a very hard time finding actual cases of voter fraud.

Indiana was the first state to implement a photo ID law, in an attempt to cut down on so-called cases of voter fraud. Indiana's precedent-setting law made its way to the Supreme Court, and when it was argued, the state was unable to cite a single specific instance of voter fraud in its entire history.

It's clear that, instead of being rampant like Republicans claim, voter fraud is virtually non-existent, no matter how hard you look.

In support of a voter ID law for his state, Kansas Secretary of State Kris Kobach cited 221 incidents of so-called voter fraud in his state between 1997 and 2010. But, as it turns out, of those 221 incidents, there were only 7 convictions, none of which were related to the impersonation of voters.

Let's move to Wisconsin, a state that Republican Party Chairman Reince Priebus once claimed was "absolutely riddled with voter fraud."

Sorry Reince. In 2004, Wisconsin's voter fraud rate was .00002 percent, or just 7 votes.

It's clear that, instead of being rampant like Republicans claim, voter fraud is virtually non-existent, no matter how hard you look.

Taxpayer Money Wasted on Voter Laws

Of course, this isn't that big of a surprise to most of us, because we've known that claims about rampant voter fraud have been false all along.

According to a study conducted by Justin Levitt of the New York University Law School, "Many of the claims of voter fraud amount to a great deal of smoke without much fire. . . . Most allegations of fraud turn out to be baseless—and that of the few allegations remaining, most reveal election irregularities and other forms of election misconduct, rather than fraud by individual voters. The type of individual voter fraud supposedly targeted by recent legislative efforts—especially efforts to require certain forms of voter ID—simply does not exist."

Millions of taxpayer dollars have been and will continue to be spent on these Republican voter suppression schemes, unless we bring an end to them.

It's time to finally put this right-wing lie to bed, and ensure that every American who has the ability to vote is able to do so.

5

Voter ID Laws Empower Marginalized Citizens

John Fund and Hans von Spakovsky

Formerly on the editorial board for the Wall Street Journal, *John Fund is currently a national affairs columnist for* National Review *and a senior editor at* The American Spectator, *a conservative political journal. He is the author of several books, including* Stealing Elections: How Voter Fraud Threatens Our Democracy. *Hans von Spakovsky is a senior legal fellow at The Heritage Foundation's Edwin Meese III Center for Legal Judicial Studies. He is a former litigator and served on the Federal Election Commission for two years. His work has appeared in the* Wall Street Journal, Washington Times, *and* National Review Online.

Voter ID laws are gaining support and polls show that the public rejects the notion that they are inherently discriminatory. Providing free photo ID to minorities will have a positive impact, empowering marginalized citizens, and will not only increase voter turnout but will safeguard the integrity of the voting system.

In one month [November 2014], voters will go to the polls to elect the entire House of Representatives and a third of the Senate. Will the midterms be clean? Could some elections

John Fund and Hans von Spakovsky, "Democrats Losing Long War Against Voter ID," *Washington Examiner*, October 6, 2014. Copyright © 2014 Washington Examiner. All rights reserved. Reproduced with permission.

be stolen? Everyone ostensibly agrees that voters have a right to know that their decision is not being ignored. And a clear majority supports a simple way to make sure: voter ID.

You would not know it if you read only the *New York Times* or watched only MSNBC, but the Left and President [Barack] Obama are losing their fight to block the widespread introduction of voter ID cards. In courts of law and the court of public opinion, the issue is gaining traction. With few exceptions, liberal pressure groups have lost lawsuits in state after state, with courts tossing out their faux claims that ID laws are discriminatory, unconstitutional or suppress minority voting.

A Majority of Americans Support Voter ID Laws

Polls show that large majorities including Republicans, Democrats, whites, blacks and Hispanics support voter ID as a common-sense reform. The myth that voter ID is a new Jim Crow-type effort to reduce minority voting is widely rejected for the rubbish that it is—except by academia and the glitterati of the mainstream media. One Rasmussen poll found that 72 percent of the public believes all voters should prove their identities before being allowed to cast ballots, and also that when it comes to voter ID, "opinions have not changed much over the years."

Many good people are mistakenly convinced that voter ID laws and other measures to buttress the integrity of elections are discriminatory.

Properly drafted voter ID laws, with safeguards against absentee ballot fraud and strict limits on laws that allow people to register and vote on Election Day, improve public confidence in elections. Even though in-person voter fraud isn't rampant, it is easy for fraudsters to commit it without getting caught. New York City's Department of Investigation last year detailed how its undercover agents claimed at 63 polling places to be individuals who were in fact dead, had moved out of town, or who were in jail. In 61 instances, 97 percent of the time, they were allowed to vote. (To avoid skewing results, they voted only for nonexistent write-in candidates.) How did the city's Board of Elections respond? Did it immediately probe and reform them sloppy procedures? Not at all. It instead demanded that the investigators be prosecuted. Most officials don't want to admit how vulnerable election systems are, but privately they express worry that close elections could be flipped by fraud.

Take Al Franken's 2008 victory over incumbent Republican Sen. Norm Coleman. A watchdog group matched criminal records with the voting rolls and discovered that 1,099 felons had cast ballots illegally. A local TV news reporter found that nine of the 10 felons he interviewed had voted for Franken. State law allows prosecutions only of those who admit knowingly committing voter fraud, and 177 were convicted. Franken's victory margin was just 312 votes. It gave Democrats their 60th Senate seat, creating the filibuster-proof majority that helped make Obamacare law.

Many good people are mistakenly convinced that voter ID laws and other measures to buttress the integrity of elections are discriminatory. Many also say fraud isn't a serious issue. Rather than fighting such laws, however, they should be working to ensure that everyone can easily obtain an ID.

Focus Should Be on Getting Proper ID, Not Opposing Voter Laws

There is sharp disagreement over how many people lack proper identification. Former Ohio Secretary of State Ken Blackwell, who is himself black, pointed out in the *Wall Street Journal* that "one of the most often-cited factoids—something that sounds authoritative but is not fact-based—is the

NAACP's claim that 25 percent of black American adults lack a government-issued photo ID. Think about that for a moment. This would mean that millions of African-American men and women are unable to legally drive, cash a check, board an airliner or participate in everyday activities of modern life." Hyperbole of this sort perpetuates the patronizing view that minorities are helpless victims. Liberals say Blackwell doesn't understand how high the barriers are for some people who lack ID. But if he were really wrong, it is difficult to see why so few voters apply for a free ID in states with such requirements.

The Right-Left stalemate can be broken. Former Presidents [Bill] Clinton and [Jimmy] Carter, at a voting summit in Texas in April [2014], endorsed the idea of adding a picture ID to Social Security cards. Carter said he would "support the idea in a New York minute." Clinton said, "The idea behind this agreement is to find a way forward that eliminates error and makes the best possible decision that we can all live with."

I cannot emphasize enough the positive impact a free and easy-to-obtain photo ID will have for those who are marginalized.

The two former presidents were joined by Andrew Young, former U.N. ambassador and confidant of Martin Luther King Jr. Young told the summit: "It is our obligation to make sure that every citizen has the ability to obtain a government-issued photo ID, and the Social Security administration is ideal for making that happen effectively and efficiently." Social Security has 1,300 offices around the country, and adding a photo option for cardholders would cost just 10 cents a card, he said.

In the Georgia state legislature in 2007, Young said voter ID was not a symbol of discrimination but a "freedom card," a natural extension of President Johnson's efforts to elevate the poor and disadvantaged. "In today's world, you can't board an airplane or get into most buildings or cash a check without predatory fees or get Medicare without a photo ID," Young said. "Ensuring people have one allows them to enter the mainstream of American life and would be a help to them."

Martin Luther King III, son of the civil rights leader, adds, "If we embrace Andy's idea, we help marginalized citizens secure independence from predators and ensure them our nation's most fundamental right to vote. My father used to talk about ending the silence of good people. I cannot emphasize enough the positive impact a free and easy-to-obtain photo ID will have for those who are marginalized."

On the other side of the political spectrum, Republicans also see promise in a photo ID Social Security card. "This would help tone down the debate over who is trying to manipulate the system and actually get real ID into the hands of whoever doesn't have one—something we should all agree on," said Don Palmer, former secretary of the Virginia Board of Elections who is now with the Bipartisan Policy Center.

Election law experts say more safeguards might be necessary to curb identity theft. The Social Security Administration warns people they should "not routinely carry your card or other documents that display your number" because "someone illegally using your number and assuming your identity can cause a lot of problems." A photo ID Social Security card would thus be limited mostly to those people without any other form of ID.

Voter ID Laws Upheld by Courts

So if both sides agree, why isn't the photo ID Social Security card already available? For one thing, Obama has been silent on the issue. White House spokesman Josh Earnest told reporters last spring that the issue was being studied. But sources say the idea is disliked both by Justice Department lawyers, who automatically oppose any voter ID requirement, and the Rev. Al Sharpton, who is helping the president find a new attorney general.

The latest big loss for voter ID opponents was in Wisconsin, where a voter ID law will be in effect for the November election. The Wisconsin Supreme Court had upheld the law against a challenge based on the state constitution in July, but it remained suspended because of an injunction issued in April [2014] by Lynn Adelman, an activist judge and former Democratic state senator. Adelman claimed it violated the 14th Amendment and the Voting Rights Act as an "unjustified burden" on the right to vote.

[Georgia's] voter ID law went into effect in 2008 after it was challenged and upheld in both federal and state court. With the law in place, voter turnout has consistently increased.

But on Sept. 12, shortly after Attorney General Eric Holder announced his intention to intervene in the lawsuit, the U.S. 7th Circuit Court of Appeals dissolved the injunction, noting in a stinging rebuke to Adelman that he had held the law invalid "even though it is materially identical to Indiana's photo ID statute, which the Supreme Court held valid in *Crawford v. Marion County Election Board.*" Adelman had even written that he did not consider the Crawford case a "binding precedent."

It was shocking to voter ID opponents that the Supreme Court's 6-3 majority decision was written not by a conservative justice but by John Paul Stevens, a liberal. The court held that Indiana's photo ID law was constitutional and did not "qualify as a substantial burden on the right to vote, or even represent a significant increase over the usual burdens of voting."

Attempts by the NAACP and the American Civil Liberties Union to persuade the Indiana Supreme Court to toss out the voter ID law also failed. Indiana's law has been in place ever since, with none of the problems that plaintiffs predicted.

It was the same in Georgia. The state's voter ID law went into effect in 2008 after it was challenged and upheld in both federal and state court. With the law in place, voter turnout has consistently increased, with 65 percent of the black voting-age population casting ballots in 2008, compared with 54.4 percent in 2004. Even without Obama on the ballot, the pattern held: While only 42.9 percent of registered black Georgians voted in 2006, 50.4 percent voted in 2010.

And Tennessee? Yes, another failure for voter ID's opponents. Tennessee's law went into effect in 2012. U.S. District Judge J. Ronnie Greer applied the rule set out by the U.S. Supreme Court, noting that "whether the plaintiff likes it or not, Crawford is the controlling legal precedent."

On the eve of the 2012 general election, South Carolina won a $3.5 million battle to protect its voter ID law against Holder's efforts to kill it. A three-judge panel dismissed the attorney general's claim that the law was discriminatory under the Voting Rights Act [VRA]. The law went into effect with no reports of problems.

Justice Department Continues to Fight Voter ID Laws

The Justice Department is also suing North Carolina and Texas over their voter ID laws. But the department suffered a setback in August when a federal judge refused to issue an injunction against North Carolina's new requirement. The Justice Department has appealed that decision and Holder may get a reversal from the 4th Circuit Court of Appeals, which Obama has stacked with liberal judges. Even if Holder wins in the 4th Circuit, however, North Carolina's law will ultimately be upheld by the U.S. Supreme Court.

The Texas case is still in court. Holder originally objected to it under Section 5 of the Voting Rights Act, claiming it was discriminatory. A federal district court in Washington, D.C., refused to dismiss his objections. But that opinion and the objection were rendered moot in 2013 when the U.S. Supreme Court, in *Shelby County v. Holder*, held that the coverage formula for Section 5 of the VRA, which dictated the state's inclusion under the Section 5 pre-clearance regime, was unconstitutional.

The trend is clear. Voter support for cleaner elections is strong and is attracting support in some Democratic states.

So the Texas voter ID law immediately went into effect for the November 2013 state elections. Contrary to the claims made in Holder's new lawsuit, which was swiftly filed under a different provision of the VRA, turnout in the 2013 election went up, not down, and there is no evidence that anyone's vote was "suppressed."

Holder, who is in his last weeks as Obama's top lawyer, has opposed election integrity measures despite clear evidence that voter ID laws do not disenfranchise voters. His mind was not changed even after a white 22-year-old videographer was able to obtain Holder's own ballot at his Washington polling place. The attorney general breezily dismissed the incident as "a stunt," ratcheted up his rhetoric and defied the nation's highest court, saying he would not "allow the Supreme Court's recent decision [in Shelby County] to be interpreted as open season for states to pursue measures that suppress voting rights."

Support for Voter ID Continues to Increase

Other states including Arizona, Alabama, Mississippi and Kansas have been able to implement their voter ID laws without hindrance. One of the few successes opponents can claim is in Pennsylvania, where the state government decided not to appeal a court decision to enjoin the state's voter ID law. This was no surprise given that the state attorney general, Kathleen Kane, a Democrat, reportedly dropped an investigation in 2013 into Democratic legislators who took bribes in exchange for votes or contracts, including opposition to the ID law. The Republican governor, Tom Corbett, who is losing his reelection battle, decided against an appeal apparently to avoid alienating liberal voters.

But the trend is clear. Voter support for cleaner elections is strong and is attracting support in some Democratic states. Rhode Island Secretary of State Ralph Mollis, a Democrat, persuaded his state's left-leaning legislature to pass a photo ID bill in 2011 to address problems of voter fraud in Providence and other cities. It included extensive outreach efforts, with members of Mollis' office going to senior centers, homeless shelters and community centers to process free IDs. The law has been implemented smoothly, Mollis says, and he views it as a national model.

"When the day is done, my job is to maintain the integrity of elections," he says. "Even if a state doesn't have an immediate problem with fraud, doesn't it make sense to take sensible precautions rather than wait for someone to abuse the system, and then it's too late?"

The same thinking might apply across the country, so that all citizens can become full participants in American life. Many on the Left and Right occupy common ground on the issue. Voter ID laws improve the honesty and efficiency of elections. They can also empower people on the margins of society.

6

Voter ID Laws Disenfranchise Minority and Poor Voters

Andrew Cohen

Andrew Cohen is an award-winning legal analyst and legal commentator, appearing frequently on 60 Minutes *and CBS Radio News. He is a fellow at the Brennan Center for Justice and contributing editor at* The Atlantic *and* The Marshall Project.

Evidence shows that the minority voter base—specifically Hispanics and economically underprivileged minorities—is steadily growing larger and could surpass the white vote in a matter of decades. Because these voters traditionally vote for Democrats, conservative groups have turned to restrictive voter ID laws as a means of suppressing the minority vote. Opponents have sought to strike down state-initiated voter ID laws on the basis of discrimination and voter suppression, claiming that such laws are an infringement against the Voting Rights Act, but this is problematic as it positions federal law against state electoral rights.

First, let's call it what it is. The burgeoning battles over state redistricting and voter ID laws—and the larger fight over a key part of the Voting Rights Act itself—are all cynical expressions of the concerns many conservatives (of both parties) have about the future of the American electorate. The Republican lawmakers who are leading the fight for the restrictive legislation say they are doing so in the name of stopping election fraud—and, really, who's *in favor* of election fraud? But the larger purpose and effect of the laws is to disenfranchise Hispanic voters, other minorities, and the poor—most of whom, let's also be clear, vote for Democrats.

Jonathan Chait, in a smart recent *New York* magazine piece titled "2012 or Never," offered some numbers supporting the theory. "Every year," Chait wrote, "the nonwhite proportion of the electorate grows by about half a percentage point—meaning that in every presidential election, the minority share of the vote increases by 2 percent, a huge amount in a closely divided country." This explains, for example, why Colorado, Nevada, and Arizona are turning purple instead of staying red. "By 2020," Chait writes, "nonwhite voters should rise from a quarter of the 2008 electorate to one third." In 30 years, "nonwhites will outnumber whites."

According to [Texas's] own data, a Hispanic registered voter is at least 46.5 percent, and potentially 120.0 percent, more likely than a non-Hispanic registered voter to lack [voter] identification.

Some States Are Making It Harder for Nonwhites to Vote

Which is why "whites," and especially white men, seem so determined this election cycle to make it harder for nonwhites to exercise their right to vote. The news from the front this week [March 2012] is telling. On Wednesday, in Pennsylvania, GOP Governor Tom Corbett raced to sign a bill that requires photo identification of voters. The day before, in Texas, GOP Attorney General Greg Abbott amended the Lone Star State's complaint against the federal government to seek to strike down the pre-clearance section of the Voting Rights Act, which had in turn been used by the Justice Department to block Texas' recent efforts at a stringent new voter-ID law.

In Wisconsin, meanwhile, a state court judge on Monday [March 12, 2015] blocked the state's new voter ID law, ruling that it unconstitutionally created a new (and lower) class of citizen-voter. Even the Human Rights Council of the United Nations has been dragged into the controversy, by the NAACP, to the great consternation of conservative bloggers and conspiracy theorists. It's all happening because lawmakers are dissatisfied with less onerous identification requirements—like those just enacted in Virginia—which allow registered voters to produce a wide range of documentation to establish that they are who they say they are.

Even though the Justice Department acted first in December [2011] in blocking a South Carolina voter-ID law, election law experts seem to agree that the Texas case is going to be the tip of the spear. Here's how the Justice Department responded when it reviewed Texas' new voter-ID law. Federal lawyers wrote:

[W]e conclude that the total number of registered voters who lack a driver's license or personal identification card issued by DPS [Department of Public Safety] could range from 603,892 to 795,955. The disparity between the percentages of Hispanics and non-Hispanics who lack these forms of identification ranges from 46.5 to 120.0 percent. That is, according to the state's own data, a Hispanic registered voter is at least 46.5 percent, and potentially 120.0 percent, more likely than a non-Hispanic registered voter to lack this identification. Even using the data most favorable to the state, Hispanics disproportionately lack either a driver's license or a personal identification card issued by DPS, and that disparity is statistically significant.

There's more. As Brentin Mock wrote earlier this week at *Colorlines*, the practical reality of life in Texas makes it difficult, if not impossible, for people who want to comply with the new ID law to do so. Mock wrote:

Texas has no driver's license offices in almost a third of the state's counties. Meanwhile, close to 15 percent of Hispanic Texans living in counties without driver's license offices don't have ID. A little less than a quarter of driver's license offices have extended hours, which would make it tough for many working voters to find a place and time to acquire the IDs. Despite this, the Texas legislature struck an amendment that would have reimbursed low-income voters for travel expenses when going to apply for a voter ID, and killed another that would have required offices to remain open until 7:00 p.m. or later on just one weekday, and four or more hours at least two weekends.

Here's how Governor Rick Perry responded:

Texas has a responsibility to ensure elections are fair, beyond reproach, and accurately reflect the will of voters. The DOJ [Department of Justice] has no valid reason for rejecting this important law, which requires nothing more extensive than the type of photo identification necessary to receive a library card or board an airplane. Their denial is yet another example of the [Barack] Obama Administration's continuing and pervasive federal overreach.

If the Voting Rights Act was originally designed to protect the rights of black Americans to vote, do we now need a new Voting Rights Act that would protect the rights of Hispanic Americans to vote?

States Claim Federal Overreach

Continuing and pervasive federal overreach. We've heard that refrain before, as constantly as a chorus in fact, since President Obama took office in 2009. Opponents of the 2010 Affordable Care Act [ACA], for example, have asserted that Congress overreached its authority under the Commerce Clause when it enacted [the ACA]. Now many of those same people say that the Justice Department is overreaching with its interpretation of the Voting Rights Act by seeking to void these state ID laws—and that the federal law itself is a statutory overreach that violates the 10th Amendment right of states to determine their own election rules.

Which brings us to Supreme Court Justice Clarence Thomas, who alone among his colleagues has expressed interest in striking down section 5 of the Voting Rights Act. In 2009, in a case styled *Northwest Austin v. Holder,* Justice Thomas memorably proclaimed "victory" in the federal war against state laws designed to disenfranchise black voters. "The constitutionality of section 5 has always depended," he wrote, "on the proven existence of intentional discrimination so extensive that elimination of it through case-by-case enforcement would be impossible. . . . 'There can be no remedy without a wrong'" (citations omitted by me).

And then Justice Thomas wrote this:

> The lack of sufficient evidence that the covered jurisdictions currently engage in the type of discrimination that underlay the enactment of § 5 undermines any basis for retaining it. Punishment for long past sins is not a legitimate basis for imposing a forward-looking preventative measure that has already served its purpose. Admitting that a prophylactic law as broad as § 5 is no longer constitutionally justified based on current evidence of discrimination is not a sign of defeat. It is an acknowledgment of victory.

So if section 5 doesn't apply to "long past sins" against black voters, what about current sins against Hispanic voters? If the Voting Rights Act was originally designed to protect the rights of black Americans to vote, do we now need a new Voting Rights Act that would protect the rights of Hispanic Americans to vote? If so, why aren't federal lawmakers tripping over themselves to get on the good side of a voting bloc that is going to increase in power over the next generation? Oh, that's right. As Chait reminds us, we are not quite yet at the point at which the benefit of shilling for Hispanic votes outweighs the burden of angering white voters.

It's unlikely new legislation is needed—we can still use the old reliable 1965 statute and apply it to new circumstances like the ones presented now. But does the discriminatory effect of state ID laws have to be so bad—"violence, terror and subterfuge" is how Justice Thomas put it—before the federal government may step in against a state? Or is it enough to establish that there is a national effort by conservative groups to press for these types of laws? (Ironic, isn't it, in a dispute conservatives argue is states' rights, that so many of these state voter ID laws would be conceived within the Beltway.)

"A Solution in Search of a Problem"

Several commentators over the past week or so have called the current generation of voter ID laws "a solution in search of a problem." But that doesn't give enough respect to the argument that we should as a nation strive to be as accurate as possible with our voting. If voting fraud is the third oldest profession, and if it is somehow rampant in all these states that have Republican leaders at their helm, then there should be reasonable ways to combat it. No responsible lawmaker ought to be against *that*. But no one seems able to find good evidence that a crisis is at hand. All Texas Attorney General Abbott could muster this week was this:

> Since 2002, the U.S. Department of Justice has prosecuted more than 100 defendants for election fraud. During the same period, election fraud investigations by the Texas Attorney General's Office have resulted in 50 convictions. Those cases include a woman who submitted her dead mother's ballot, a paid operative who cast two elderly voters' ballots after transporting them to the polling place, a city council member who unlawfully registered ineligible foreign nationals to vote in an election that was decided by a 19-vote margin, a Starr County defendant who voted twice on

Election Day, a Harris County man who used his deceased father's voter registration card to vote in an election, a worker who pled guilty after attempting to vote for two of her family members, and a Brooks County man who presented another voter's registration card and illegally cast that voter's ballot on Election Day.

In 10 years, just 100 federal prosecutions and 50 state convictions—in a colossal state with a population of more than 25 million people. You can do the math. You can be stupid and vote in America. You can be drunk and vote in America. You can be mentally insane and vote in America. You could vote in America for Snooki or Rod Blagojevich. Or, like tens of millions of your fellow citizens, you can choose not to vote at all. But if you don't have the means to get a driver's license, or if you cannot afford the time and money it takes to get certain other forms of government ID, you are out of luck? What a great country this is.

Biometric Solutions Should Be Pursued to Replace Voter ID Cards

Robert A. Pastor

Robert A. Pastor was a former member of the National Security Council, a presidential advisor, and a specialist in Latin American diplomacy and US foreign policy. A respected professor and author and editor of numerous books on foreign affairs, Pastor passed away in 2014.

Biometric identification is an ideal bipartisan solution that would assuage Republicans' concern for electoral integrity while also building Democrats' confidence in a fair and free vote for all citizens. This technology—which has already been adopted by Mexico—could also prove to be an effective means to verify migrant status and differentiate undocumented workers from legal residents.

The American people want the Democratic and Republican parties to solve our nation's problems together, but bipartisan solutions become possible only if each side gives the other the benefit of the doubt. We should begin with two polarizing issues—voter fraud and migration. Biometric identification cards offer a solution for both.

More than 30 states require identification cards to vote. Republicans believe such ID cards are important to prevent electoral fraud. Democrats believe voter impersonation is not a problem, and that the real reason for the IDs is to suppress the votes of poor and old people and minorities, who lack cards and tend to vote Democratic.

The Supreme Court accepted that voter identification cards were a legitimate instrument for ensuring ballot integrity, but many state courts suspended the laws because they were implemented late with confusing rules and without easy access to cards. In fact, statewide IDs are of little help because most cases of double voting are by people with homes in two states.

Free National Biometric ID Cards

The solution to the problem is for Democrats to accept that voter IDs are important, and for Republicans to accept that all eligible voters should receive free national biometric cards, which would have unique identifiers for each person based on fingerprints or an iris scan.

Democrats suspect the real reason [Republicans oppose amnesty] is that Republicans fear the new immigrants will vote Democratic.

In the 1990s, Mexico provided biometric IDs to all of its citizens in just three years, using Kodak and IBM technology. Mexicans now use them for many purposes. If the U.S. were to provide such a card to all citizens, it would address Republican concerns about ballot integrity while assuring Democrats that everyone would have a card and could vote. Indeed, the process could add as many as 50 million eligible but currently unregistered people to voter rolls.

A dividend to this bipartisan solution is that it could also solve the most vexing part of the immigration issue. Because of the growing importance of the Latino vote, both parties want to move forward on immigration, and a small bipartisan group in the Senate has gained some agreement on border enforcement and greater access for high-skilled immigrants and low-skilled agricultural workers. This initiative and the president's ideas are positive and encouraging signs of compromise, but they don't solve the problem. And their ideas for addressing the hardest issue—legalization for the 11 million undocumented workers in the U.S.—are unlikely to make it through the congressional gantlet.

Democrats favor legalization because they believe it would be wrong to divide families or deport 11 million people. Republicans oppose amnesty because they fear that after the economy recovers, a new wave of illegal migration will begin, much as occurred after the 1986 immigration reform. Democrats suspect the real reason is that Republicans fear the new immigrants will vote Democratic.

Biometric ID Can Also Help Solve the Illegal Immigration Problem

The first step toward resolving this is for each side to give the other the benefit of the doubt. The Democrats should accept the Republican concern of the unintended effect of amnesty, and Republicans should accept the Democratic opposition to mass deportations.

There is a way to permit legalization without opening the floodgates. Although the U.S. has invested about $187 billion since 1986 to stop illegal migration at its borders or to deport those in the country, the borders can never be fully secure. The flaw in the system is in the workplace. The U.S. has relied on a system to check workers' identities and residency—E-Verify—that is flawed, voluntary and used in few states.

The solution for elections—a biometric ID—would also help solve the illegal migration problem. With systematic and effective verification for all workers, undocumented people would not find work and would not come. Legal residents, who are not citizens, would have a card that would allow them to work but not vote.

A comprehensive immigration solution should not only include legalization and a workplace ID card but also a North American investment fund to narrow the income gap between Mexico—the source of the vast majority of migrants—and the United States. The fund would connect North America with better transportation and infrastructure, promoting growth in Mexico that would reduce the incentive for people to migrate. As our second-largest market, Mexico's growth is also good for us.

A biometric card has a permanent and unique means of identifying each person and therefore cannot be hacked or forged. More and more countries are using it. In the U.S., it is already used in passports; the FDA [Food and Drug Administration] uses it to combat fraud in the food stamp program; and Disney World takes biometric information from guests' fingerprints to ensure that a multi-day ticket is used by the same person. Some fear that a national ID could be used improperly, but arbitrary abuse is far more likely if there are multiple, flawed IDs rather than a single, secure one.

It would not be easy or cheap to implement, but Mexico did it, and the U.S. can too. To assuage concerns, the president and Congress could set up a group to propose ways to ensure privacy, prevent identify theft and address any other concerns. Acting on these two issues in this way could not only prove bipartisanship is possible, it could solve two vexing issues.

Allowing Noncitizens to Vote Is the Right Thing to Do

Ron Hayduk

Ron Hayduk is professor of political science at Queens College in New York and cofounder of the Coalition to Expand Voting Rights. He is the author of Democracy for All: Restoring Immigrant Voting Rights in the United States *and has contributed to a wide variety of journals on the subject of voting rights.*

Historically, the right to vote in America has not been tied to citizenship status but rather to residency. There are millions of immigrants residing in the United States who pay taxes and contribute to society, but who are unfairly prohibited from the democratic process simply because they are noncitizens. This situation is unfair, and thus resident noncitizens should be allowed to vote.

The contemporary immigrant rights movement has commanded attention through civil disobedience, student walkouts and intensive lobbying. But there's another tactic— increasing immigrant clout by allowing all noncitizens to vote—that also deserves serious consideration.

Many Americans understandably question why immigrants should be able to vote before they become U.S. citizens. They know citizenship is required for federal elections, and they attested to their status when they registered. But what most don't know is that the right to vote in this country has never been intrinsically tied to citizenship. And even now, in a few jurisdictions and on some issues, noncitizens have a limited right to vote.

As it turns out, voting by noncitizens is as old as the Republic. From 1776 until 1926 in 40 states and federal territories, residents who weren't citizens could vote in local, state and sometimes federal elections. They also have held public office; Indiana and Louisiana elected noncitizen aldermen and coroners, for example. In a country where "no taxation without representation" was the rallying cry for revolution, and where government theoretically rests "on the consent of the governed," allowing all residents to vote only makes sense.

Noncitizens Contribute in Many Ways but Lack a Political Voice

Today, immigrants here legally and illegally work in every sector of the economy. They own homes and businesses, attend colleges and send children to schools. They pay billions in taxes each year, and make countless social and cultural contributions to their communities. They are subject to all the laws that govern citizens, serve in the military and even die defending the U.S. But most are without formal political voice.

Noncitizens suffer social and economic inequities, in part, because policymakers can ignore their interests. The vote is a proven mechanism to keep government responsive and accountable to all.

Their numbers are staggering. According to the U.S. Census Bureau, more than 22 million adults in the U.S. are barred from voting because they lack U.S. citizenship. In some districts—and in some whole cities and towns—noncitizens make up 25 percent to 50 percent of voting-age residents. In Los Angeles they make up more than one-third of the voting-age population; in New York City, they are 22 percent of adults.

Such levels of political exclusion approximate the exclusion of women prior to 1920, African Americans before the Voting Rights Act of 1965 and 18-year-olds prior to 1971.

Sadly, America knows all too well what can occur when groups don't have a formal political voice: discriminatory public policy and private practices—in employment, housing, education, healthcare, welfare and criminal justice.

Noncitizens suffer social and economic inequities, in part, because policymakers can ignore their interests. The vote is a proven mechanism to keep government responsive and accountable to all.

But why don't they just become citizens? Most immigrants want to, but the average time it takes for the naturalization process is eight years and sometimes longer. That's a long time to go without a vote.

Besides, many who are here legally are barred from pursuing citizenship by the terms of their visas; they are students or green card holders who are nonetheless members of their community who deserve a voice in its policies. And, of course, those who are here illegally, who overstayed a visa or never had one have no practical pathway to citizenship.

Residency Requirements Should Not Disenfranchise Noncitizens

But do noncitizens possess sufficient knowledge of our political system to vote responsibly? If political knowledge was a criterion for voting, many U.S. citizens would be out of luck, as public surveys regularly show. Moreover, as it is, a citizen can move from New York to Los Angles and register and vote within 30 days, even if he or she doesn't know a thing about the candidates or ballot proposals. So why should literacy tests or restrictive residency requirements be able to disenfranchise noncitizen voters?

There are now a handful of U.S. jurisdictions where noncitizens have a right to vote in some elections. In six towns in

Maryland since the 1990s, all residents (except felons serving sentences or those judged mentally incompetent by a court) can vote in local elections. Chicago permits all noncitizen parents of schoolchildren to vote in local school council elections. In California, all parents can participate in "parent trigger" votes to change the administration of their children's schools.

Next year, the New York City Council will take up a bill—which has broad political support—that would allow noncitizens lawfully residing in the U.S. to vote in local elections. In March, Burlington, Vt., voters will decide on a similar ballot proposition to let legal permanent residents vote in local elections. The District of Columbia has a similar bill pending.

The right to vote helps keep our democracy inclusive and fair, and resident voting is the next logical step toward creating a truly universal franchise. It is what America's past and future as an immigrant nation requires. Noncitizen voting is the suffrage movement of our time.

State Laws Should Be Amended to Allow Ex-Felons to Vote

Eric Holder

Eric Holder was the first African American to serve as attorney general of the United States. During his tenure, which ran from 2009 to 2015, Holder fought to defend the Voting Rights Act of 1965 and took a strong public stance against voter ID laws. He has also received several awards for his work as a private attorney.

The US Department of Justice's Smart on Crime initiative is a key component to reforming the criminal justice system. Former prisoners who have paid their debt to society should be free to participate in the electoral process like all other American citizens. Felony re-enfranchisement encourages civic participation and rehabilitation, whereas denying former prisoners this freedom is counterproductive and unjust.

Today, we gather in recognition of the fact that, although our laws and procedures must be continually updated, our commitment to the cause of justice must remain constant. From its earliest days, our Republic has been bound together by its extraordinary legal system, and by the enduring values that define it. These values—of equality, opportunity, and justice under law—were first codified in our founding

Eric Holder, "Attorney General Eric Holder Delivers Remarks on Criminal Justice Reform at Georgetown University Law Center," United States Department of Justice, February 11, 2014. Courtesy of justice.gov.

documents. And they are put into action every day by leaders like you—and the talented men and women who learn, at great institutions like Georgetown [University], what it means to be a steward of the law—and an advocate for those whom it protects and empowers.

Although the issues on our agenda this morning are difficult and at times divisive, the diversity of this crowd—and the panelists and Members of Congress you'll be hearing from—is a testament to the fact that criminal justice reform is essentially not a partisan issue. It's about providing legal professionals and law enforcement leaders with the 21st-century solutions they need to address 21st-century challenges. It's about shaping a system that deters and punishes crime, keeps us safe, and ensures that those who pay their debts have the chance to become productive citizens. Most importantly, it's about answering fundamental questions—about fairness and equality—that determine who we are, and who we aspire to be, not only as a nation, but as a people—a people resolved to move forward together, and committed to implementing criminal justice policies that work for everyone in this country.

We're partnering with state officials, agency leaders, and others . . . to advance proven strategies to help formerly incarcerated people successfully rejoin their communities.

DOJ's "Smart on Crime" Initiative

This is the challenge—and the extraordinary opportunity—that brings us together this morning. And it's the same challenge that drove me, roughly one year ago, to launch a targeted Justice Department review of our criminal justice system: to identify areas for improvement and make this system as efficient, as effective, and as just as possible.

Last August [2013], I announced a new "Smart on Crime" initiative—based on the results of this review—that's already allowing the Justice Department to strengthen the federal system; to increase our emphasis on proven diversion, rehabilitation, and reentry programs; and to reduce unnecessary collateral consequences for those seeking to rejoin their communities. Among the key changes we're implementing is a modification of the Department's charging policies—to ensure that people who commit certain low-level, nonviolent federal drug crimes will face sentences appropriate to their individual conduct—rather than stringent mandatory minimums, which will now be reserved for the most serious criminals.

As you'll be discussing later today, this change will not only make our system fairer—it will also make our expenditures more productive. It will enhance our ability to combat crime, reduce drug-fueled violence, and protect our communities. And it will complement proposals like the bipartisan Smarter Sentencing Act—cosponsored by Senators Dick Durbin, Mike Lee, and Chairman Patrick Leahy, along with Representatives Bobby Scott and Raul Labrador—to give judges more discretion in determining appropriate sentences for those convicted of certain crimes.

As we work with Members of Congress to refine and pass this legislation, my colleagues and I are simultaneously moving forward with a range of other reforms. We're investing in evidence-based diversion programs—like drug treatment initiatives and veterans courts—that can serve as alternatives to incarceration in appropriate cases. We're working to target law enforcement resources to the areas where they're needed most. And we're partnering with state officials, agency leaders, and others—including members of the Federal Interagency Reentry Council, comprised of Cabinet Secretaries and leadership from throughout the [Barack] Obama Administration—to advance proven strategies to help formerly incarcerated people successfully rejoin their communities.

After all, at some point, 95 percent of all prisoners will be released. And just as we expect everyone who commits a crime to pay their societal debts, we also expect them to remain sober and crime-free upon their release. We expect them to get jobs and find housing. And we expect them to become productive, law-abiding members of society.

Formerly incarcerated people continue to face significant obstacles. . . . And in far too many places, their rights— including the single most basic right of American citizenship—the right to vote—are either abridged or denied.

Unfortunately, as you know all too well, these expectations are not always met. Rates of recidivism remain unacceptably high. And that's why the Smart on Crime initiative is driving us to tear down unnecessary barriers to economic opportunities and independence. I've directed every United States Attorney to designate a Prevention and Reentry Coordinator in his or her district to ensure that this work will be a top priority throughout the country. And I've ordered our law enforcement components, and asked state Attorneys General, to reconsider policies that impose overly burdensome collateral consequences on formerly incarcerated individuals without meaningfully improving public safety.

Former Prisoners Must Become Productive Members of Society

This is important because we've seen that maintaining family connections, developing job skills, and fostering community engagement can reduce the likelihood of re-arrest. And we know that restoring basic rights—and encouraging inclusion in all aspects of society—increases the likelihood of successful reintegration. We've taken significant steps forward in improving reentry policies and addressing the unintended collateral consequences of certain convictions.

Yet formerly incarcerated people continue to face significant obstacles. They are frequently deprived of opportunities they need to rebuild their lives. And in far too many places, their rights—including the single most basic right of American citizenship—the right to vote—are either abridged or denied.

However well-intentioned current advocates of felony disenfranchisement may be—the reality is that these measures are, at best, profoundly outdated.

As the Leadership Conference Education Fund articulated very clearly in your recent report, "there is no rational reason to take away someone's voting rights for life just because they've committed a crime, especially after they've completed their sentence and made amends." On the contrary: there is evidence to suggest that former prisoners whose voting rights are restored are significantly less likely to return to the criminal justice system. As your report further notes, a study recently conducted by a parole commission in Florida found that, while the overall three-year recidivism rate stood at roughly 33 percent, the rate among those who were re-enfranchised after they'd served their time was just a third of that.

Unfortunately, the re-enfranchisement policy that contributed to this stunning result has been inexplicably and unwisely rolled back since that study was completed. And, in other states, officials have raised hurdles to be faced by those with past convictions seeking to regain their access to the ballot box. And that's why I believe that, today—starting here and now—it is time for criminal justice leaders to come together to address this issue. It is time to fundamentally reconsider laws that permanently disenfranchise people who are no longer under federal or state supervision.

These restrictions are not only unnecessary and unjust, they are also counterproductive. By perpetuating the stigma and isolation imposed on formerly incarcerated individuals, these laws increase the likelihood they will commit future crimes. They undermine the reentry process and defy the principles—of accountability and rehabilitation—that guide our criminal justice policies. And however well-intentioned current advocates of felony disenfranchisement may be—the reality is that these measures are, at best, profoundly outdated. At worst, these laws, with their disparate impact on minority communities, echo policies enacted during a deeply troubled period in America's past—a time of post-Civil War repression. And they have their roots in centuries-old conceptions of justice that were too often based on exclusion, animus, and fear.

History of Felony Disenfranchisement

The history of felony disenfranchisement dates to a time when these policies were employed not to improve public safety, but purely as punitive measures—intended to stigmatize, shame, and shut out a person who had been found guilty of a crime. Over the course of many decades—court by court, state by state—Americans broadly rejected the colonial-era notion that the commission of a crime should result in lifelong exclusion from society.

After Reconstruction, many Southern states enacted disenfranchisement schemes to specifically target African Americans and diminish the electoral strength of newly-freed populations. The resulting system of unequal enforcement—and discriminatory application of the law—led to a situation, in 1890, where ninety percent of the Southern prison population was black. And those swept up in this system too often had their rights rescinded, their dignity diminished, and the full measure of their citizenship revoked for the rest of their lives. They could not vote.

In the years since, thanks to the hard work, and the many sacrifices, of millions throughout our history, we've outlawed legal discrimination, ended "separate but equal," and confronted the evils of slavery and segregation. Particularly during the last half-century, we've brought about historic advances in the cause of civil rights. And we've secured critical protections like the Civil Rights Act of 1964 and the Voting Rights Act of 1965.

Yet—despite this remarkable, once-unimaginable progress—the vestiges, and the direct effects, of outdated practices remain all too real. In many states, felony disenfranchisement laws are still on the books. And the current scope of these policies is not only too significant to ignore—it is also too unjust to tolerate.

Millions of Americans Are Denied the Right to Vote

Across this country today, an estimated 5.8 million Americans—5.8 million of our fellow citizens—are prohibited from voting because of current or previous felony convictions. That's more than the individual populations of 31 U.S. states. And although well over a century has passed since post-Reconstruction states used these measures to strip African Americans of their most fundamental rights, the impact of felony disenfranchisement on modern communities of color remains both disproportionate and unacceptable.

Eleven states continue to restrict voting rights, to varying degrees, even after a person has served his or her prison sentence and is no longer on probation or parole.

Throughout America, 2.2 million black citizens—or nearly one in 13 African-American adults—are banned from voting because of these laws. In three states—Florida, Kentucky, and Virginia—that ratio climbs to one in five. These individuals and many others—of all races, backgrounds, and walks of life—are routinely denied the chance to participate in the most fundamental and important act of self-governance. They are prevented from exercising an essential right. And they are locked out from achieving complete rehabilitation and reentry—even after they've served the time, and paid the fines, that they owe.

Fortunately—despite unfortunate steps backward in a few jurisdictions, and thanks to the leadership of policymakers from both parties and criminal justice professionals like you—in recent years we have begun to see a trend in the riqht direction. Since 1997, a total of 23 states—including Nebraska, Nevada, Texas, and Washington State—have enacted meaningful reforms. In Virginia, just last year, former Governor McDonnell adopted a policy that began to automatically restore the voting rights of former prisoners with non-violent felony convictions.

These are positive developments. But many of these changes are incremental in nature. They stop well short of confronting this problem head-on. And although we can be encouraged by the promising indications we've seen, a great deal of work remains to be done. Given what is at stake, the time for incrementalism is clearly over.

Eleven states continue to restrict voting rights, to varying degrees, even after a person has served his or her prison sentence and is no longer on probation or parole—including the State of Florida, where approximately 10 percent of the entire population is disenfranchised as a result. In Mississippi, roughly 8 percent of the population cannot vote because of past involvement with the criminal justice system. In Iowa, action by the governor in 2011 caused the state to move from automatic restoration of rights—following the completion of a criminal sentence—to an arduous process that requires direct intervention by the governor himself in every individual case. It's no surprise that, two years after this change—of the 8,000 people who had completed their sentences during that governor's tenure—voting rights had been restored to fewer than 12.

Restrictive Voting Laws for Former Prisoners Are Unjust

That's moving backwards—not forward. It is unwise, it is unjust, and it is not in keeping with our democratic values. These laws deserve to be not only reconsidered, but repealed. And so today, I call upon state leaders and other elected officials across the country to pass clear and consistent reforms to restore the voting rights of all who have served their terms in prison or jail, completed their parole or probation, and paid their fines.

I call upon experts and legislators to stand together in overturning an unfortunate and outdated status quo.

And I call upon the American people—who overwhelmingly oppose felony disenfranchisement—to join us in bringing about the end of misguided policies that unjustly restrict what's been called the "most basic right" of American citizenship.

Permanent exclusion from the civic community does not advance any objective of our criminal justice system.

I applaud those who have already shown leadership in raising awareness and helping to address this issue. Later today, this conference will hear from Senator Rand Paul, who has been a leader on this matter. His vocal support for restoring voting rights for former inmates shows that this issue need not break down along partisan lines.

Bipartisan support will be critical going forward because, even in states where reforms are currently taking hold, we need to do even more. And we need to make sure these positive changes are expanded upon—and made permanent.

Virginia's progress has come through the executive power of its former governor, rather than the legislature—meaning that, without action by state lawmakers, these reforms can be reversed by any future executive with the stroke of a pen. More broadly, the inconsistent patchwork of laws affecting felony disenfranchisement varies so widely between states—and, in some places, between cities and counties—that even those who administer the laws are sometimes unfamiliar with how to apply them. *The New York Times* noted in 2012 that this kind of confusion means that many who are legally allowed to vote erroneously believe that their rights are restricted. And too often, those who do understand their rights are wrongfully turned away.

Disenfranchisement Does Not Advance the Criminal Justice System

Today—together—we need to correct this injustice. As the evidence has shown, and as I pointed out in an amicus brief—filed more than a decade ago, in a case challenging Florida's disenfranchisement law—permanent exclusion from the civic community does not advance any objective of our criminal justice system. It has never been shown to prevent new crimes or deter future misconduct. And there's no indication that those who have completed their sentences are more likely to commit electoral crimes of any type—or even to vote against pro-law enforcement candidates.

What is clear—and abundantly so—is that these laws sever a formerly incarcerated person's most direct link to civic participation. They cause further alienation and disillusionment between these individuals and the communities that our Smart on Crime policies encourage them to rejoin. And particularly at a time when our prisons are overflowing—and many who are serving sentences for nonviolent drug crimes find themselves trapped in a vicious cycle of poverty and incarceration—it is counterproductive to exclude these individuals from the voting franchise once their involvement with the corrections system is at an end. It is contrary to the goals that bring us together today. And it is not consistent with the cherished ideals that once led Supreme Court Justice William Brennan to call disenfranchisement "the very antithesis of rehabilitation."

Whenever we tell citizens who have paid their debts and rejoined their communities that they are not entitled to take part in the democratic process, we fall short of the bedrock promise—of equal opportunity and equal justice—that has always served as the foundation of our legal system. So it's time to renew our commitment—here and now—to the notion that the free exercise of our fundamental rights should never be subject to politics, or geography, or the lingering effects of flawed and unjust policies.

After all, at its most basic level, this isn't just about fairness for those who are released from prison. It's about who we are as a nation. It's about confronting—with clear eyes, and in frank terms—disparities and divisions that are unworthy of the greatest justice system the world has ever known. It's about ensuring that we hold accountable those who do wrong—while preserving the values our nation has always held sacred. And it's about protecting the American people and strengthening our communities—while enabling all of our citizens, no matter who they are or where they're from, to make their voices heard.

Throughout America's long history of progress, struggle, and sacrifice—as generation after generation has come together to move our nation closer to the ideals our founders envisioned, and to advance our pursuit of a more perfect Union—this country has always looked to its legal system to answer questions of right and wrong; of truth and justice.

This morning, these questions remain before us—and the pursuit of a more perfect Union goes on. Although I recognize, as you do, that the progress we seek will not be easy—and the reforms we need will not take hold overnight—I am proud to join and, where necessary, lead, this bipartisan group in seeking solutions to these urgent issues. I am honored to count you as colleagues in the work of forging a more just society that reflects our conviction that all are created equal. And despite the difficulties, the opposition, and the resistance we will undoubtedly face—as I look around this room—I cannot help but feel confident in where today's experts, and tomorrow's leaders, will take us in the months and years to come.

10

Felons Lose Their Right to Vote When They Break the Law

Roger Clegg

Roger Clegg has served extensively in government as both the former deputy assistant attorney general and assistant to the solicitor general in the Ronald Reagan and George H.W. Bush administrations. He is the current president and general counsel of the Center for Equal Opportunity, a conservative organization dedicated to eradicating racism and ethnic discrimination.

Granting felons the right to vote should be a case-by-case decision, not blanket legislation. The argument that felon disenfranchisement laws are racist is unfounded, and neither the US Constitution nor the Voting Rights Act afford felons voting rights. Felons deserve to pay the consequences for their crimes and should not automatically be given the right to vote.

It makes sense that felons should lose their right to vote. You don't have a right to make the laws if you aren't willing to follow them yourself. To participate in self-government, you must be willing to accept the rule of law.

We don't let everyone vote—not children, not noncitizens, not the mentally incompetent. There are certain minimum and objective standards of trustworthiness, responsibility, and commitment to our laws that we require before people are en-

Roger Clegg, "Building the Case: In Opposition to Felon Voting Rights," *Bothsides,* January 22, 2015. Copyright © 2015 Christiannewswire. All rights reserved. Reproduced with permission.

trusted with a role in the solemn enterprise of self-government. Those who have committed serious crimes against their fellow citizens don't meet those standards.

This doesn't mean that the right to vote should never be restored to felons, but the decision to restore the right to vote should not be made automatically. It should be made carefully, on a case-by-case basis, weighing the seriousness of the crime, how long ago it was committed, and whether there is a pattern of crime.

If a felon shows that he or she really has turned over a new leaf and is no longer a threat to the community, but is giving something back to it, then it makes sense to restore the right to vote to that individual. A formal ceremony, with a federal judge and the felon's family and friends present, would be appropriate and meaningful then.

The people whose voting rights will be diluted the most if criminals are allowed to vote are the law-abiding people in high-crime areas, who are themselves disproportionately black and Latino.

But it should not be done automatically. The restoration of the right to vote then is not meaningful, and it is not wise. After all, two out of three felons who are released from prison commit another crime, and it is ridiculous to assert that the reason they do so is that they can't vote.

Arguments Allowing Felons to Vote Are Unpersuasive

The other arguments made in favor of felons voting are also unpersuasive.

For example, it's frequently asserted that, once he's been released from prison, a felon has "paid his debt to society." It's true that he's paid enough of his debt to be allowed out of prison, but that doesn't mean there aren't continuing consequences. We don't let felons possess firearms or serve on juries, for instance. By the way, most of the groups that want felons to be able to vote want them to be able to vote when they are still in prison, so this "paid their debt to society" argument is a red herring.

It's also often asserted that felon disenfranchisement laws are "racist." That's not true either. To be sure, they may have a disproportionate impact on some racial groups, because at any point in time there are always going to be some groups that statistically commit more crimes than others, but that doesn't make the laws racist—just as the fact that more crimes are committed by men doesn't make criminal laws sexist. The people whose voting rights will be diluted the most if criminals are allowed to vote are the law-abiding people in high-crime areas, who are themselves disproportionately black and Latino.

As a historical matter likewise, it's not true that these laws have racist roots. While a few southern states passed such laws a hundred years ago, those statutes are no longer on the books, and they would be unconstitutional if they were. Today's laws haw their roots in ancient Greece and Rome, came to the American colonies from England, and are found in nearly every state in the country, where they were adopted without any racist intent at all and have never been applied discriminatorily.

If there were persuasive evidence that these laws are racially discriminatory, then there are plenty of well-funded organizations—starting with the U.S. Department of Justice—that would be eager to bring lawsuits against them. The fact that such lawsuits are not being brought shows that the evidence of racial discrimination is just not there.

The Supreme Court has ruled that as a general matter these laws do not violate the Constitution, and indeed the Constitution itself contains language approving of felon disenfranchisement. Similarly, the history of the Voting Rights Act makes clear that it was not intended to require letting criminals vote.

Finally, remember again that the people who are the victims of crime are themselves disproportionately poor and minority. It does them no good to empower criminals; rather, it serves them, the rest of society, and indeed felons themselves best if we create incentives for individuals to show they have turned over a new leaf before they are re-empowered. Automatic felon re-enfranchisement sends a bad message: We do not consider criminal behavior such a serious matter that the right to vote should be denied because of it.

People can be forgiven, but that does not mean there aren't consequences for wrongdoing. And requiring evidence of repentance before easing those consequences makes perfect sense.

Gerrymandering Is a Form of Legal Voter Fraud

Harry McAlevey

Harry McAlevey is a recent graduate of McGill University and writes for Daily Kos, *a liberal political blog, and for* The Political Bouillon, *a university collective independent journal.*

Gerrymandering—the redrawing of congressional districts to favor one political party or the other—threatens democracy and disenfranchises voters, and Republicans are largely to blame for using such systematic tactics to obstruct the electoral process. Independent, nonpartisan voting commissions should be given control of redistricting—not biased politicians.

In any representative democracy, changes in population and territory necessitate redistricting, so as to give equal value to all voters. This idea, popularly known as "one person, one vote," is crucial for the preservation and promotion of true democracy. Unfortunately, the people who decide exactly how to best draw a district are politicians, who are less concerned with proper representation and more concerned with holding onto their power. The problem of rigging the redistricting process in favor of a certain party, candidate, or incumbent, is known as "gerrymandering," and it is arguably the largest threat to democracy currently facing the United States.

Harry McAlevey, "Gerrymandering and the Art of Legal Election Fraud," *Daily Kos*, May 9, 2014. Courtesy of 2014 Daily Kos. All rights reserved. Reproduced with permission.

Minority Voters Are Disenfranchised in the Current System

In a perfect system, each district would be exactly the same. In a country of a million people with one hundred districts, each district would have 10,000 people, with the same per capita representation of minorities, women, and economic disparities. Obviously this is not possible, especially in a nation as diverse and with such a controversial history as the United States; the next best option, then, is to strive to meet that perfect system as strongly as possible. Yet the current map is full of discrepancies and errors, with minority voters often disenfranchised and districts that weave and wind like a snake without any coherency or rationality.

To be sure, the Democratic Party is not exempt from using gerrymandering to their advantage; but more often than not it is Republicans who use a widespread, systematic program to disenfranchise voters.

Redistricting happens every ten years, in a convoluted process that is supposedly based off the results of the census. Gerrymandering districts is not a complicated process; it only requires drawing of districts in such a way that hostile voters are "packed" into one district, giving the opposition a landslide in that district while turning another, traditionally safe district into a competitive one. Incumbents utilize gerrymandering to stay in power, and they have been using it more and more often as the electorate rapidly diversifies.

The midterm election of 2010, arguably the largest disaster in Democratic Party history, had far more implications than most thought. The switch of House control to Republicans was devastating for national Democrats, but state legislatures also swung hard to the right. This gave Republicans a chance to control much of the redistricting process across the country. The result? While Democratic candidates in the House won the nation-wide election by over 1.4 million votes, Republicans took a 33-seat majority.

To be sure, the Democratic Party is not exempt from using gerrymandering to their advantage; but more often than not it is Republicans who use a widespread, systematic program to disenfranchise voters. With a diversifying electorate beginning to sour to obstructionist, outdated conservative politics, [Republican strategist] Karl Rove and others sought new ways for the GOP to retain its power. The Republican State Leadership Committee created such a program, the Redistricting Majority Project (REDMAP), which according to the header on their website "fight[s] for a fair process." Yet the rest of the website flaunts their ability to disenfranchise voters, including in Pennsylvania, which reelected [Barack] Obama by more than five points but, due to heavy investment in 2010, sent 13 Republicans to the House, compared to only 5 Democrats. This rigging of the system is not limited to any specific state or region. Republicans have been so good at packing districts that, with current districts in place, Democrats would have to win the popular vote by 7 percentage points to take a majority in the house.

Redistricting Should Be Controlled by an Independent Commission

No one can claim the current system is functioning properly. Moreover, this is not an issue that can be kicked down the road, and dealt with in future generations. Reducing the impact of a vote reduces the interest of the voter, shrinking an already pitifully small electorate and creating widespread apathy. Allowing elected officials to essentially choose who is elected perpetuates a system rife with inefficiency, complacency, and dysfunction. Change needs to come now.

Control of the redistricting process should immediately be taken out of the hands of politicians and given to independent electoral commissions. Allowing state legislatures to map out congressional districts is an abhorrent idea, with any hope for non-bias being ludicrous. These non-partisan groups can use advanced software and data to accurately map out the country according to demographic statistics, pushing us closer to the ideal system mentioned earlier. No district can look exactly like another; urban areas in Detroit will never resemble the plains of Nebraska. But they can even the playing field and ensure that, as best as possible, one person's vote is equivalent to any others. The fact that this has to be fought for is appalling in and of itself, but it is something worth fighting for.

The current political system in America is a disaster: the House is rigged and unfixable until 2020 (the next census), the Senate is incapable of action because 41 senators are apparently equivalent to 59, and the president has essentially turned into a lame duck. Those in office are typically out-of-touch or corporate panhandlers, and party elites stifle the few seeking to actually make a difference. Pessimistic as it may seem, it is unfortunately the realistic picture. The change has to come from the people, who, at the very least, can vote into office the people they think can make a difference. That is, if their vote actually counts.

12

US Primary System Disenfranchises Millions of Voters

Chad Peace

Chad Peace is a lawyer, a legal strategist for the Independent Voter Project, and managing editor for IVN, an online political news and policy organization.

Most elections are won during the primaries and do not represent the will or intent of the general state population, but rather that of interest groups and private political parties, which the primary system is set up to protect. Elections should benefit citizens and reflect their majority vote, not just pander to powerful political party members.

Our American election system is broken in no small part thanks to the primary election system. The Republican and Democratic parties have worked hand-in-hand for over a century to make "their" party primaries the centerpiece of the entire electoral process.

In an age where 43 percent of Americans consider themselves politically independent of the two major parties, the twisted state-sanctioned closed primary election process prevalent in the majority of U.S. elections frequently leads to election results that are patently warped.

The parties have managed to subvert the will of the electorate, generally, through a combination of clever redistricting (read: gerrymandering), as well as artful rewriting of state electoral laws in every state.

Consequently, across America, unpopular candidates with party-line doctrinaire positions routinely "win" (occupy) "safe" seats in general elections simply by pandering exclusively to the increasingly narrow-minded interest groups whose influence is magnified as the partisan voter bases decrease. This is because over 90 percent of elections are now "decided" during the primary stage of the election process.

Elections should serve voters. So every voter, regardless of party, should have a say before an election is "decided" for anyone.

Why Political Parties Control Elections

For example, Ted Cruz was elected to the U.S. Senate in 2012 by virtue of his winning the Republican Party primary in Republican-dominated Texas. The number of votes he actually received from the electorate in that primary represented less than 4 percent of the total vote in Texas.

Similarly, Hillary Clinton was re-elected to the U.S. Senate in 2006 by virtue of winning the Democratic Party primary in Democratic-dominated New York. The number of votes she actually garnered in that critical primary election represented less than 5 percent of the total vote in New York.

Would these two candidates have won in a more competitive election? Maybe. But that's not the point. Elections should serve voters. So every voter, regardless of party, should have a say before an election is "decided" for anyone.

Nationally, the privatized primary election process will determine the field of "legitimate" candidates for the presidential election in November 2016.

For example, significant public interest and media attention will give inordinate weight to the few voters in New Hampshire who control the outcome of its early primary. Yet, this massively influential bloc of voters represents less than 0.01 percent of the total estimated US vote!

State legislatures at the turn of the 20th century instituted publicly-funded primary elections as an attempt to democratize the candidate nomination process. Since that time, the parties have slowly reframed election laws through legislatures and courtrooms to protect the party power structure from competition at the ballot box.

While parties have a private right to nominate candidates, and thereby preclude non-members from their voting process, the states and the federal government have a much larger constitutional obligation to provide all voters, not just party members, a meaningful opportunity to participate in our election process on a level playing field.

In other words, the individual political rights of every citizen cannot be infringed upon because a private political party has been given an unfair advantage.

The State of New Jersey argued in favor of this exclusionary process, despite the fact that 47 percent of voters in New Jersey are registered as unaffiliated.

The U.S. Supreme Court in *California Democratic Party v. Jones* (2000), for example, held that party primaries are private affairs, and therefore the state cannot force political parties to allow nonmembers to participate.

But the fact of the matter is that these supposedly private, closed party primaries are openly administered and promoted by most states, and are almost always funded by taxpayers.

In an effective and constitutional response to the outlawing of legally-mandated open primaries, voters in California and Washington states have adopted nonpartisan blanket primaries, which have all voters, candidates, and parties compete on the same ballot under the exact same rules. Party affiliation is irrelevant under the eyes of the law in those states.

An Overview of How Primary Elections Work

On March 17, 2015, a legal challenge to New Jersey's closed primary system was heard in the Third Circuit Court of Appeals in *Balsam, et al. v. Guadagno (New Jersey Secretary of State).*

In oral argument in that case, the attorney for the State of New Jersey said that the rights of political parties to control "their" primary elections outweighed the interests of individual voters to participate in the election process on an equal playing field with Republicans and Democrats. The State of New Jersey literally said that voters who feel disenfranchised should simply join one of the two parties, or work hard to find a candidate of their own and go through a petition process to get them on the ballot.

The State of New Jersey argued in favor of this exclusionary process, despite the fact that 47 percent of voters in New Jersey are registered as unaffiliated. The state maintained that the exclusive nature of its primary elections is therefore not a question for the federal courts.

New Jersey's argument, and the Third Circuit's opinion in the state's favor, seems absurd when placed in a historical context.

In the 1940s, African-Americans challenged the constitutionality of the primary election system in Texas because the Democratic Party would not let them vote in this integral stage of the electoral process (*Smith v. Allwright*).

In that case, the Democratic Party made the same flawed argument that the State of New Jersey and the Third Circuit upheld in the current case. It argued that its primaries are private affairs and that African-Americans' right to vote is unaffected because they could vote in the general election.

In 1944, the Supreme Court held that, because the Democratic Party's primary served an important state function, the state could not in effect preclude African-Americans from voting under the Fifteenth Amendment because party rights do not trump the right of individual voters to be adequately represented.

In the 1960s, for example, both major political parties used a gerrymandering tactic called mal-apportionment to insulate themselves from competition within districts. In Republican-controlled states, the Republicans did it. In Democratic controlled states, the Democrats did it.

In brief, the party in power would draw some districts larger by population to effectively dilute the influence of voters in the opposition party. In defense of the mal-apportionment practice, both political parties and the state legislatures they controlled vigorously argued that the federal courts did not have jurisdiction to get involved in the apportionment of districts because it was a "political question" to be addressed within a state.

Elections should be conducted for the benefit of every citizen, to elect representatives that truly represent their district, their state, and their country.

But in 1962, the Supreme Court in *Baker v. Carr* held that the Constitution protected the "political right" associated with the right to vote, and clearly distinguished this "right" from a political "question." Then, in 1963, the Supreme Court in *Gray v. Sanders* determined that the practice of mal-apportionment was unconstitutional, and first articulated the now famous "one person-one vote" standard. Of significant note, *Gray v. Sanders* concerned the right to vote in a primary election.

The following year, the Supreme Court applied the same standard to a litany of similar cases challenging malapportionment all over the country in *Reynolds v. Sims.*

Elections Should Benefit Citizens Not the Political Parties

The decision to uphold New Jersey's exclusionary primary election, handed down by the Third Circuit Court of Appeals just a few weeks after oral argument, is perhaps testament to how high the hurdles have been raised for individual voters to participate equally in a political institution that has been controlled by political party insiders for so long.

But it's really this simple: elections should be conducted for the benefit of every citizen, to elect representatives that truly represent their district, their state, and their country. Such elections would make government more accountable to the people, decrease the influence of narrow interest groups, and ironically, strengthen the parties by forcing them to broaden their message.

Today, American elections don't do that.

And that's simply not right.

13

The Broken US Voting System Is an Assault on Voting Rights

Election Protection and Lawyers' Committee for Civil Rights Under Law

Election Protection is a nonpartisan voter protection coalition that provides voters with the information they need to have a voice in the electoral process. The Lawyers' Committee for Civil Rights Under Law, a nonpartisan, nonprofit organization, provides legal services in support of racial equality.

Millions of votes have been lost in recent years due to a multitude of problems in the election system, such as faulty equipment, poorly trained poll workers, and inaccurate voter rolls. New voter ID laws, intended to deter fraud, only make matters worse and do little to address the real causes behind the nation's faltering voting system. Both litigation and legal field monitoring services, such as provided by Election Protection, help to identify and resolve voting problems and secure the integrity of the democratic process.

Every year, countless Americans across the country are blocked from voting—many having done everything they were supposed to do to exercise their civic right. For these eligible and qualified voters—who show up at the polls on Election Day to make their voices heard only to be turned away because they inexplicably do not appear on the voter rolls or encounter a poorly trained poll worker not following voting rules—our democracy is broken.

The tragedy is that these problems are not new. The deficiencies in our election system became painfully obvious following the 2000 Presidential election, when Americans witnessed in Florida how administrative blunders can undermine voting rights and have such consequential implications. In 2004 in Ohio, mismanagement of the election was so severe that a federal court found tens of thousands of Ohio voters had been disenfranchised as a result. In 2008, it was clear that our system of voter registration was in desperate need of modernizing when, according to the 2008 Survey of the Performance of American Elections, a joint report issued by CalTech and the Massachusetts Institute of Technology, approximately 2.2 million votes were lost because of registration problems.

Despite [the] chronic problems already experienced by voters, in 2011 and 2012 state lawmakers flooded legislatures across the country with new voting rules.

Voters Experienced Numerous Problems at the Polls in 2012

The complications for voters in 2012 were not different in form from previous elections. Intractable problems with access to the ballot and ineffective planning for and implementation of elections reinforced for many voters a lack of confidence in the integrity of the voting process. These problems, which are recurrent and systemic, include:

- Voter registration errors

- Ineffective planning

- Misallocation of resources and voting equipment

- Undertrained poll workers misapplying rules and not following proper procedures

- Understaffed polling places

- Malfunctioning voting machines

- Problems with absentee ballots

- Mismanaged polling locations

- Deceptive election practices

One voter from Florida stood in line for three hours only to be told that her name was not on the voter roll despite her certainty that she registered at the Department of Motor Vehicles. At an early voting site in Georgia, a voter reported waiting in line for eight hours even though half of the voting machines at that site were not being used, because there were only two poll workers checking in voters, which clogged the line. In Cleveland, hundreds of voters who had requested absentee ballots did not receive them because they were erroneously marked as "not registered." In Michigan, several hundred absentee ballots were lost in the mail and, despite being aware of the problem, the local clerk did not attempt to notify the voters about their lost ballots or resend them. In Detroit, there was chaos and hours of delay at polling places with multiple precincts assigned to them because voters did not know which line to stand in and no poll worker was directing voters to their correct precinct line. Voters essentially had to guess which line to stand in at the risk of waiting for hours in the wrong line.

New Voting Laws Exacerbated Existing Problems

Yet, despite these chronic problems already experienced by voters, in 2011 and 2012 state lawmakers flooded legislatures across the country with new voting rules, all of which seemed to have the same effect on voting: creating more barriers and decreased access. These legislators prioritized restrictive photo identification laws—forms of identification less likely to be possessed by the elderly, African-Americans, veterans, Latinos, students, people with disabilities, and lower income voters. Cuts to early voting opportunities were also on lawmakers' agenda as were new restrictions on voter registration. These laws were passed in the name of protecting election integrity, yet the real problems that burden voters were completely ignored.

In addition to state actors, anonymous groups began efforts earlier than ever to deceive and intimidate voters.

In fact, the new voting changes exacerbated existing pitfalls in the voting process. The rapid pace of the voting law changes, combined with the lack of preparation for responsible implementation, increased the confusion and problems voters experienced on Election Day. Reduced early voting opportunities intensified polling place congestion. New voter identification laws caused a great deal of voter confusion and were widely misapplied by poll workers who were confused about what was acceptable identification, which added to wait times and forced too many eligible voters to vote provisionally.

The assault on voters did not end in state legislatures. State election officials in Florida, Colorado, and Texas undertook statewide programs to purge voters from the voter rolls based on faulty data matches that incorrectly ensnared eligible American citizens. In one case, a World War II veteran received wide public attention after his county election supervisor sent him a letter incorrectly telling him that he was not a U.S. citizen. Voters were also subject to mass challenges by individuals affiliated with a Tea Party group called "True the Vote" who, in states like North Carolina and Ohio, frivolously challenged voters' eligibility prior to Election Day by using faulty software developed by the organization. Though many of the challenges were unsupported and dismissed, some voters were compelled to attend hearings to defend their eligibility to vote against baseless accusations. These additional encumbrances added unnecessary strain to under-resourced local election officials and were a distraction from the real tasks required to run elections.

In addition to state actors, anonymous groups began efforts earlier than ever to deceive and intimidate voters. Voters in numerous states received robocalls giving them wrong polling place information. In Florida and Virginia voters received calls incorrectly informing them that they could vote by phone. In Ohio and Wisconsin, billboards were erected in predominantly minority communities warning of criminal penalties associated with voter fraud.

Steps Taken to Protect Voters

Despite these setbacks, the 2012 election demonstrated yet again that Americans will continue to overcome barriers to exercise their right to vote, and they were not without assistance. After witnessing the challenges of the 2000 presidential election, civil rights organizations and the legal community mobilized to create Election Protection, which today is the nation's largest non-partisan voter protection coalition. The coalition consists of more than 100 organizations and thousands of attorney volunteers dedicated to ensuring that every eligible American who wants to vote is able to cast a ballot. The 2012 elections marked the third Presidential election that Election Protection played a vital role supporting and protecting voters.

The centerpiece of the program incorporates three national Election Protection Hotlines: the English language 1-866-OUR-VOTE, administered by the Lawyers' Committee for Civil Rights Under Law; the Spanish language 1-888-VEY-VGTA, administered by National Association of Latino

Elected and Appointed Officials Educational Fund; and this year's pilot Asian language hotline 1-888-API-VOTE, administered by Asian American Justice Center and APIA Vote. Voters around the country call the Hotlines for live assistance from trained volunteers who provide information and help to resolve voting problems.

Modern American elections require an overhaul of our voter registration system, which is woefully out-of-date and continues to be the biggest and most persistent cause of Election Day problems.

In addition to the Hotlines, in 2012 Election Protection organized on-the-ground legal field monitoring operations in 22 states: Arizona, California, Colorado, Florida, Georgia, Illinois, Louisiana, Maryland, Massachusetts, Michigan, Minnesota, Missouri, New Mexico, New York, Nevada, North Carolina, Ohio, Pennsylvania, South Carolina, Texas, Virginia, and Wisconsin. Through a partnership with Common Cause, the National Coalition on Black Civic Participation, and the Conference of National Black Churches, the program supplemented its legal field program with grassroots volunteers which expanded polling monitoring coverage across the country. By working collaboratively with local election officials, Election Protection was able to bring attention to voting issues as they arose and troubleshoot to resolve voting problems.

Litigation was also exceptionally important to combating many of the new state laws that would have otherwise burdened or disenfranchised voters. Federal voting laws, such as Section 5 of the Voting Rights Act and the National Voter Registration Act, proved indispensable in states such as South Carolina, Florida, and Texas, where successful litigation mitigated the effects of the suppressive laws.

US Voter Registration System Needs to Be Overhauled

Over the course of 10 years, Election Protection has collected hundreds of thousands of reports from voters in all 50 states that paint the true picture of American elections. With this one-of-a-kind data, we are able to identify the causes of endemic voting problems and develop solutions to deal with them effectively. First and foremost, modern American elections require an overhaul of our voter registration system, which is woefully out-of-date and continues to be the biggest and most persistent cause of Election Day problems, including the overuse of provisional ballots, long lines, and outright disenfranchisement. A modern voter registration system will make our elections more convenient, inexpensive, and efficient and will allow communities to reinvest resources now absorbed by voter registration in other critical functions. No less critical, it is imperative that election officials plan effectively. Proper resource allocation, poll worker recruitment and training, polling place management, and contingency planning are critical to running fair elections and must be thoughtfully planned out in advance of Election Day. Additionally, increased access to voting such as expanded early voting opportunities and no-excuse absentee voting can help alleviate Election Day congestion. Finally, deceptive election practices must be criminalized to protect voters against those who intentionally spread false election information for the purpose of disenfranchising voters. . . .

The assault on voting rights was a stark reminder that some Americans have had to continually fight against barriers to attain and exercise their right to vote. Although the time in our history has passed when certain Americans were excluded by force of law from electoral participation, endemic yet solvable problems continue to plague our system of elections and prevent too many eligible voters from fully participating in our democracy. Barriers continue to exist through state laws designed by politicians to make it difficult for certain Americans to vote and administrative deficiencies that impair voting rights. These perennial institutional barriers to the vote must be addressed for they are the cause of the long lines that were rampant throughout the election cycle. The 2012 elections was a clarion call for change and it is urgent that lawmakers answer this call and finally tackle these issues in a meaningful way.

14

Online Voting Is Promising but Will Need Transparency to Avoid Fraud

Tom Risen

Tom Risen writes about business, technology, and national security for U.S. News & World Report. *He has been published in the* National Journal, Slate, *and* Government Executive *and has also appeared as a commentator on the BBC and Huff Post Live.*

While online voting is already practiced in many smaller European nations, its progress in the United States has been thwarted by international data breeches, consumer data hacks, and major corporate cybersecurity attacks. Many Americans believe that even standard voting processes are insecure and subject to fraud. Cybersecurity legislation and information transparency can help to increase voters' confidence in online voting systems.

B oth elections and the Internet reached a new level in 2004. The launch of Facebook and growth of Myspace created a new era of social networks, while the controversial, wartime presidential campaign popularizing "red and blue" state terms for the political leanings of voters. People wondered how those milestones might change America by 2014.

Democratic Processes

2004 prediction: *By 2014, network security concerns will be solved and more than half of American votes will be cast online, resulting in increased voter turnout.*

Some at the time hoped that because of new technology more than half of all U.S. votes would be cast online by 2014, according to a survey conducted a decade ago by the Pew Internet Project. Those people were also asked to predict whether all network security concerns would be solved by 2014—but only 32 percent agreed both milestones would be reached by this year, while 50 percent of the respondents disagreed with or challenged the idea. History has unfortunately proven the cynics right on both issues.

Networks Remain Insecure

Far from Pew's hopeful prediction of last decade this past year set a new record for data breaches of company customer information and international theft of trade secrets by hackers sponsored by Russia and China. Breaches of customer data at retailers like Target and banks like JPMorgan Chase were caused because companies were unprepared for cybersecurity challenges.

Americans may need to get more involved in the campaign process before they become motivated enough to cast Internet ballots in large numbers.

Approximately 47 percent of U.S. adults have had their information stolen by such hacks, and that rate will likely increase as mobile device use increases, according to a study conducted by CNNMoney and the Ponemon Institute, a cybersecurity research firm. Despite these risks only 31 percent of U.S. businesses have a security strategy for the rapidly growing mobile sector, and less than half of American companies have taken enough precautions to protect consumer data, according to the PricewaterhouseCoopers' 2014 U.S. State of Cybercrime Survey.

Online Voting Never Took Off

Some form of online voting exists in 30 states, but the Internet has not become the main way people choose their leaders—in part because cybersecurity never made it to the next level either. The National Institute of Standards and Technology still warns that online voting has cybersecurity risks.

Even in 2004 Internet voting had trouble gaining momentum. The military began testing the Secure Electronic Registration and Voting Experiment in 2004 to allow service members stationed overseas vote online in the general election, but Deputy Defense Secretary Paul Wolfowitz canceled that plan after government-commissioned studies warned about the cybersecurity flaws in the system. Since then many of the 30 or so states that offer online voting options have taken grants from the Pentagon's Federal Voting Assistance Program to help develop those systems, McClatchy reports.

Online voting could boost election turnout but in a chicken or the egg irony it seems that Americans may need to get more involved in the campaign process before they become motivated enough to cast Internet ballots in large numbers.

The Internet definitely influenced how we decide to vote but it has not changed how we vote dramatically enough to reshape American democracy.

Election turnout in the U.S. remains low in recent years despite efforts by get-out-the-vote nonprofits since the close presidential races of 2000 and 2004. The overall voter turnout for eligible Americans rose from 47.1 percent in 2000 to 51.6 percent in 2004 and 53.3 percent in 2008, according to the U.S. Census Bureau. Turnout in midterm elections remains even lower, with 34.8 percent of voting age Americans casting their ballot in 2002, followed by 36.1 percent in 2006 and 37 percent in 2010.

Fears of voter fraud also remain a partisan argument adding to criticism that online voting is unsecure and unreliable. Americans must show a form of voter identification at the polls according to laws in 34 states, according to the National Conference of State Legislatures. Opponents of such laws including the American Civil Liberties Union say there is little fraud of this kind, and those rules may actually restrict the right to vote for low-income Americans that cannot afford identification like a driver's license or passport.

Building a Secure, Digital Democracy by 2025?

The Internet definitely influenced how we decide to vote but it has not changed how we vote dramatically enough to reshape American democracy. President Barack Obama sailed to victory in the 2008 election by mobilizing voters using social networks and new digital data collection software that was easy for his campaign volunteers to use. On the dark side YouTube made it easy for a video of Sen. George Allen, R-Va., saying racial slurs to go viral online and contribute to his defeat in the 2006 election. Twitter also helped people in Tunisia and Egypt share information about large protests that would upend governments in 2011, so the growth of social networks is a bright spot for supporters of online voting. Congress is well aware of the need for more cybersecurity but remains divided on a solution. Lawmakers including Sen. Dianne Feinstein, D-Calif., will likely continue to push for cybersecurity legislation, including laws to notify customers when their data is compromised in a hack, but success depends on whether the next Congress remains deadlocked.

Transparency seems like a step forward to a better internet voting system and cybersecurity. Cybersecurity information sharing between companies and government is accepted among both political parties as a start on the path to preventing large scale hacks—Congress just needs to agree long enough to compromise and pass a bill. That could in turn inspire more faith in online voting systems. Voting using the Internet and mobile devices has become mainstream in smaller nations including Estonia and Switzerland, so there is hope for larger nations like America to cast more e-ballots.

15

Experts Believe Online Voting Is Inevitable

Sam Smith

Sam Smith is a reporter and editor at The Christian Post. *He has written for a number of news outlets, including Patch.com and Maryland Reporter.com.*

Internet voting is the way of the future and would likely increase voter turnout, specifically among absentee voters. Individual state election laws vary and, as a result, not all citizens have equal access to voting. Removing as many barriers to the process, such as modernizing the system, could also help increase the youth vote.

Democrats and Republicans agreed that Internet voting is "inevitable" for the future of America's election process at a panel hosted by the University of Maryland's Center of American Politics and Citizenship on Capitol Hill Wednesday [September 12, 2012].

"Its just a matter of time until people demand that we vote on the Internet. People do everything on the internet," said Republican Dave Mason, a former commissioner of the Federal Election Commission.

Would Online Voting Actually Get More People to Vote?

Democrat Bob Carey, former director of the Federal Voting Assistance Program [FVAP], said that online voting would likely lead to a higher voting turnout. He said that at the very least it guarantees more military votes would be counted.

"In the 2010 election, there were approximately 220,000 military voters, who would have otherwise voted if they had the same voter participation rate as the rest of the population," Carey said. "I've been out at sea. It takes two, three, four weeks to get a letter. We always had Internet access. We have printers on board. We can easily get those ballots out there. When I was at FVAP, I strongly advocated online voting."

The prospect of online voting would certainly introduce new security and fraud risks.

Although Mason supports online voting, he said he does not feel that online voting would lead to increased voter participation. Other efforts made to increase voter turnout, such as early voting, have not lead to more votes.

Mason also noted that online voting would change the way in which candidates and parties will have to appeal to the voters.

"There is a big social difference in the way that we govern ourselves," Mason said. "It will change the nature of voter appeal, the kinds of appeals that we make towards voters when they make the decision at their computer."

New Security and Fraud Risks in Online Voting

State Voter ID laws have made voting fraud a hot-button issue that Republicans see as important and Democrats view as insubstantial. The prospect of online voting would certainly introduce new security and fraud risks.

But Carey said that although there are risks associated with an online voting system, there are security risks associated with any voting system, especially the current system pointing out the debacle in the extraordinarily close 2000 presidential election.

"You can essentially eliminate the possibility of someone being able to hack into a Virtual Private Network [VPN] and change a ballot. Can someone hack into a VPN? Sure. Can they hack into a VPN without being detected? Virtually impossible," Carey said. "I really do believe that full Internet voting is something that we eventually need to get to. This is something that definitely needs to be discussed, funded, researched, developed and deployed."

Mason said that the major threat in an Internet system is not likely to come from hackers, but from how easy it will be to influence the votes and possibly pay off voters.

Making It Easier to Vote

With just 41.7% of eligible voters casting a ballot in the 2010 elections, the panel discussed ways in which the voting process can be made less difficult.

"When you look at the percentage of people that vote knowing what people have gone through to get to vote, is very discouraging," said Laura Still Thrift, senior legislative assistant for U.S. Rep. David Price, a North Carolina Democrat.

As an American citizen, it distresses me that people of California have more access to voting than someone in Delaware, or that someone in Tennessee is less likely to vote than someone in Oregon.

Difficulties for voters largely depend on the individual state's election laws. Marty Stone, a former member of the Democratic Congressional Campaign Committee, said that it's easier to vote in some states than others because of strict absentee ballot laws.

In states such as Virginia and Tennessee, voters that wish to cast absentee ballots must provide a legal reason to vote through the mail. States such as California and more recently, Maryland do not require an excuse to vote through the mail.

Better Access to Voting in Some States than Others

"As an American citizen, it distresses me that people of California have more access to voting than someone in Delaware, or that someone in Tennessee is less likely to vote than someone in Oregon," Stone said.

Thrift mentioned that Price has co-sponsored a number of bills that would make it easier for people to cast their vote.

One bill would prohibit the requirement for photo identification, a new mandate in some states. Another would permit same-day voter registration so that people don't have to take time in advance to register. Another one would ensure that if a state allows you to vote by mail, it would allow everyone to vote by mail.

Thrift also discussed measures in which the registration process could be modernized. For example, allowing people to register when they have any interaction with the federal government and requiring colleges to educate out-of-state students on the state's voting laws so the students can change their residency.

"This is pushing back against efforts that make it harder and more difficult to vote," Thrift said.

However, as Mason said during the earlier Internet voting discussion, making voting easier will not guarantee an increased turnout.

"One of the remarkable things to me when looking at voting statistics as we have taken down barriers to vote and made it easier to register, expanding the franchise, voter participation rates have not tended to go up," Mason said. "In fact, in some cases there have been a slight negative result."

Organizations to Contact

The editors have compiled the following list of organizations concerned with the issues debated in this book. The descriptions are derived from materials provided by the organizations. All have publications or information available for interested readers. The list was compiled on the date of publication of the present volume; the information provided here may change. Be aware that many organizations take several weeks or longer to respond to inquiries, so allow as much time as possible.

Advancement Project
1220 L St. NW, Suite 850, Washington, DC   20005
(202) 728-9557 • fax: (202) 728-9558
website: www.advancementproject.org

Advancement Project is a multiracial grassroots organization founded by civil rights lawyers in 1999 to reform unjust policies for communities of color and promote racial justice and equality. It provides local support and legal council for communities seeking social justice as well as offers a variety of education, communications, and training resources to help influence democracy and advocate reform on a national level. Advancement Project's website includes links to reports on a variety of advocacy issues, including voting rights for minorities.

America Votes
1155 Connecticut Ave. NW, Suite 600, Washington, DC   20036
(202) 962-7240 • fax: (202) 962-7241
e-mail: info@americavotes.org
website: www.americavotes.org

America Votes collaborates with over four hundred local and national partners to advocate for and advance voting rights in the United States. Founded in 2003, America Votes is a progressive organization that seeks to advance electoral reforms such as voter protection and expanded ballot access. It also convenes the annual "America Votes State Summit," featuring political strategists and experts who help to forecast electoral challenges and examine potential solutions.

American Civil Liberties Union (ACLU)

125 Broad St., 18th Floor, New York, NY 10004
(212) 549-2500
e-mail: infoaclu@aclu.org
website: www.aclu.org

Founded in 1920, the American Civil Liberties Union's (ACLU) mission is to preserve, protect, and defend the basic liberties guaranteed by the US Constitution and the Bill of Rights. As a nonprofit, nonpartisan organization with over five hundred thousand members, it is the largest public interest law firm in the nation and brings more than six thousand cases to court annually. The ACLU seeks to address all issues that threaten American civil liberties, including voter fraud and suppression, gerrymandering, and criminal re-enfranchisement.

Brennan Center for Justice at New York University (NYU) School of Law

161 Avenue of the Americas, 12th Floor, New York, NY 10013
(646) 292-8310 • fax: (212) 463-7308
e-mail: brennancenter@nyu.edu
website: www.brennancenter.org

Named after notable US Supreme Court Justice William J. Brennan Jr., the Brennan Center for Justice at New York University School of Law is a nonpartisan law and policy organization dedicated to holding the government accountable to the US Constitution. With offices in New York City and Washington, DC, the Center conducts research, drafts policies, and advocates in the courts on issues such as voting rights, constitutional protections, and campaign finance reform.

Fair Elections Legal Network (FELN)

1825 K St. NW, Suite 450, Washington, DC 20006

(202) 331-1550
e-mail: info@fairelectionsnetwork.com
website: www.fairelectionsnetwork.com

The Fair Elections Legal Network (FELN) was founded by a group of lawyers committed to defending the accessibility and integrity of the electoral process. FELN employs attorneys who seek to improve the voting process for all Americans, with a specific emphasis on representing students and minorities. FELN also advocates for voting rights by providing training for organizations and by collaborating with local and state public officials. FELN's website offers a variety of election reform resources including fact sheets, state-specific voting guides, and an overview of its Campus Vote Project, an initiative that educates students about their voting rights.

FairVote
6930 Carroll Ave., Suite 610, Takoma Park, MD   20912
(301) 270-4616
e-mail: info@fairvote.org
website: www.fairvote.org

FairVote is a nonprofit, nonpartisan organization that seeks to strengthen American democracy by ensuring that all Americans are given a fair vote. The organization advocates for reform in three key areas: fair representation, fair elections, and fair access. FairVote also publishes a variety of research reports, policy perspectives, and strategies at its website that examine improvements and solutions for the American electoral system. It also provides traditional high schools with a proprietary voting curriculum, Learning Democracy, which encourages students to participate in the democratic process.

The Heritage Foundation
214 Massachusetts Ave. NE, Washington, DC   20002
(202) 546-4400
e-mail: info@heritage.org
website: www.heritage.org

The Heritage Foundation is a conservative think tank that conducts policy research and presents its findings to Congress, policy officials, and members of the academic community. Established in 1973, the Foundation is dedicated to promoting its core conservative policy principles through three organizational institutions: The Institute for Economic Freedom and Opportunity; The Institute for Family, Community and Opportunity; and The Kathryn and Shelby Cullom Davis Institute for National Security and Foreign Policy. Its website includes published research, testimonies by public policy experts, fact sheets, multimedia presentations, and lectures by leading scholars and politicians. Many of these deal with the issue of voter fraud.

League of Women Voters (LWV)
1730 M St. NW, Suite 1000, Washington, DC   20036
(202) 429-1965 • fax: (202) 429-0854
website: www.lwv.org

The League of Women Voters (LWV), which grew out of a convention of the National American Woman Suffrage Association in 1920, was established to educate and encourage women to use their hard-won right-to-vote as a means to influence politics and government. As a nonprofit, nonpartisan organization, LWV strives to inform and engage citizens in policy and legislation issues and advocates for fair voting rights for all Americans. It has over eight hundred local and national leagues as well as international leagues in Hong Kong and the US Virgin Islands.

National Voting Rights Institute (NVRI)
27 School St., Suite 500, Boston, MA   02108
(617) 624-3900 • fax: (617) 624-3911
e-mail: nvri@nvri.org
website: www.nvri.net

The National Voting Rights Institute (NVRI) is a Boston-based nonprofit organization dedicated to ensuring that all Americans have the right to participate in the democratic process. Through a formal collaboration with the public policy organization Demos, NVRI works to reform campaign spending limits, protect the right to vote, and raise public funding for elections. The organization also initiates litigation on electoral finance matters, as well as US citizen enfranchisement. Its website includes links to videos, press releases, and other articles about their work.

Pew Research Center

1615 L St. NW, Suite 700, Washington, DC   20036
(202) 419-4300 • fax: (202) 419-4349
website: www.pewresearch.org

Pew Research Center is a nonprofit, nonpartisan research organization that conducts a wide variety of social science research such as demographic studies, global and regional trend reports, and public opinion polling. Established in 2004 as a subsidiary of The Pew Charitable Trusts, the Pew Research Center publishes a wide range of data-driven reports, articles, and interactives on its website that are authored by the Center's subject matter experts. Some of these deal with the issue of voter fraud and voter ID and other laws being implemented across the United States.

Project Vote

805 15th St. NW, Suite 250, Washington, DC   20005
(202) 546-4173 • fax: (202) 733-4762
website: www.projectvote.org

Project Vote provides underrepresented, low-income, and minority voters with the resources and education they need to participate in the electoral process. As a nonprofit, nonpartisan organization, Project Vote employs a variety of strategies to expand access to the ballot, such as litigation, advocacy, and research. The organization's Get Out the Vote program helps register voters in frequently disenfranchised communities. It also provides information on voting issues through publications at its website and blog.

Rock the Vote

1001 Connecticut Ave. NW, Suite 640, Washington, DC 20036
(202) 719-9910
e-mail: info@rockthevote.com
website: www.rockthevote.com

Rock the Vote's mission is to mobilize and educate young adults to become a central voice in the electoral process. Using a revolutionary combination of music, pop culture, and technology to reach new voters, Rock the Vote holds voting drives, advocates for voting rights, and employs a variety of cutting-edge strategies to register millennials to vote. A nonprofit, nonpartisan organization, Rock the Vote's website provides a wealth of information to help inform, inspire, and equip young people to engage in political discourse.

Southern Coalition for Social Justice

1415 West Hwy. 54, Suite 101, Durham, NC 27707
(919) 323-3380 • fax: (919) 323-3942
website: www.southerncoalition.org

The Southern Coalition for Social Justice, based in Durham, North Carolina, exists to challenge and defend against the racism and discrimination of ethnic minorities, immigrants, and people of color. The organization encourages civic participation by working to safeguard minority electoral rights and seeks to advance the causes of environmental and criminal justice as well as immigrant rights. As a nonprofit organization, it also provides legal aid and advocacy to disadvantaged and minority communities.

True the Vote

PO Box 131768, Houston, TX 77219
e-mail: info@truethevote.org
website: www.truethevote.org

True the Vote is a citizen-led, nonpartisan initiative dedicated to preventing voter fraud and preserving the integrity of the electoral process. The organization is committed to ensuring a fair and free election through a variety of technology tools, including The Knowledge Network, an online tool that helps volunteers connect and communicate voter fraud prevention efforts, and VoteStand, a smart phone app that enables voters to report electoral abuse immediately when they see it happen. True the Vote's website assists citizens with obtaining voter ID and provides them with a way to report inaccurate voter registry records through its National Voter Registration Analysis tool. The organization also provides education and support to volunteers in all fifty states.

US Election Assistance Commission (EAC)
1335 East West Hwy., Suite 4300, Silver Spring, MD   20910
(866) 747-1471 • fax: (301) 734-3108
website: www.eac.gov

The US Election Assistance Commission (EAC) is an independent, bipartisan governmental agency that provides election officials with the resources they need to implement voting reforms, technologies, and systems. Established by the Help America Vote Act of 2002 (HAVA), EAC is responsible for maintaining the national mail voter registration form, testing and certifying voting equipment, and distributing federal funds to states as imposed by HAVA. A team of senate-confirmed commissioners, who are held accountable to their duties by Congress, leads the commission, which also serves as a national clearinghouse for election administration information, research, and data.

Verified Voting
PO Box 4104, Carlsbad, CA   92018
(760) 434-8683 • fax: (760) 841-1880
website: www.verifiedvoting.org

Verified Voting, a nonprofit lobbying organization, works to enforce the integrity of the electoral process by ensuring that voting systems are secure, reliable, and accurate. The organization pairs technology experts with election legislators and officials to ensure that online and electronic voting systems are auditable. Its sister organization, the Verified Voting Foundation, is committed to safeguarding the democratic process by educating the public about the need for accurate and transparent voting systems. The Foundation's website is home to Voting News, which includes a blog, national news, and editorial articles dedicated to raising awareness for voting and electoral fraud issues.

Voto Latino

PO Box 18416, Washington, DC   20008
(202) 386-6374
e-mail: info@votolatino.org
website: www.votolatino.org

Voto Latino strives to engage Latino millennials in the political issues that impact their lives and communities by giving them a voice in the electoral process. The organization, both nonpartisan and nonprofit, cultivates civic understanding and responsibility by mobilizing Latino voters to participate in US elections. Recognizing that Hispanics comprise less than 10 percent of the technology workforce in America, Voto Latino champions the Innovator's Challenge, a competition created to spur Latino young people toward careers in technology. Voto Latino's website also provides a page where registrants can receive updates on President Barack Obama's executive action on immigration, as well offers as an online voter registration tool.

Bibliography

Books

R. Michael
Alvarez, Triad E.
Hall, and Susan
D. Hyde, eds.

Election Fraud: Detecting and Deterring Electoral Manipulation. Washington, DC: Brookings Institution Press, 2008.

Donathan L.
Brown and
Michael L.
Clemons

Voting Rights Under Fire: The Continuing Struggle for People of Color. Santa Barbara, CA: Praeger, 2015.

Richard J. Ellis
and Michael
Nelson, eds.

Debating Reform: Conflicting Perspectives on How to Fix the American Political System. Washington, DC: CQ Press, 2011.

Erik J. Engstrom

Partisan Gerrymandering and the Construction of American Democracy. Ann Arbor: University of Michigan Press, 2013.

John Fund

Stealing Elections: How Voter Fraud Threatens Our Democracy. San Francisco: Encounter Books, 2004.

John Fund and
Hans von
Spakovsky

Who's Counting?: How Fraudsters and Bureaucrats Put Your Vote at Risk. New York: Encounter Books, 2012.

Richard L. Hasen

The Voting Wars: From Florida 2000 to the Next Election Meltdown. New Haven, CT: Yale University Press, 2012.

Ron Hayduk   *Democracy for All: Restoring Immigrant Voting Rights in the United States.* New York: Routledge Taylor & Francis Group, 2006.

Alexander Keyssar   *The Right to Vote: The Contested History of Democracy in the United States.* New York: Basic Books, 2000.

Gary May   *Bending Toward Justice: The Voting Rights Act and the Transformation of American Democracy.* New York: Basic Books, 2013.

Lorraine C. Minnite   *The Myth of Voter Fraud.* Ithaca, NY: Cornell University Press, 2010.

Periodicals and Internet Sources

Michael Agresta   "Will the Next Election Be Hacked?," *Wall Street Journal,* August 17, 2012.

Laura Lee Baris   "Stopping Voter Fraud Without So-Called Racist Voter ID Laws," *People's Pundit Daily,* November 8, 2014. www.peoplespunditdaily.com.

Gene Berardelli   "Hard Evidence Supports the Need for Voter ID Laws," IVN, January 16, 2014. www.ivn.com.

Nick Bilton   "Disruptions: Casting a Ballot by Smartphone," *New York Times,* November 11, 2012.

Jamelle Bouie   "The Most Brazen Attempt at Voter Suppression Yet," *Slate,* October 29, 2014. www.slate.com.

DiversityInc   "Is Jim Crow Back? Racist Voter Laws
                    Exclude 5 Million Blacks, Latinos
                    from Polls," October 23, 2012.
                    www.diversityinc.com.

Kevin Drum   "The Quick Way to End the
                    Voter-Fraud Wars? A National ID
                    Card," *Mother Jones*, July/August
                    2012.

David A.   "Selling Votes Is a Common Type of
Fahrenthold   Election Fraud," *Washington Post*,
                    October 1, 2012.

John Fund   "Voter Fraud: We've Got Proof It's
                    Easy," *National Review*, January 12,
                    2014. www.nationalreview.com.

Jeremiah Goulka   "Are Voter ID Laws a Form of
                    Racism?," *Mother Jones*, October 15,
                    2012.

Meagan   "31 in a Billion: Election Expert's
Hatcher-Mays   Report Shatters Right-Wing Media
                    Voter ID Myths," Media Matters for
                    America, October 24, 2014.
                    www.mediamatters.org.

Christopher   "7 Papers, 4 Government Inquiries, 2
Ingraham   News Investigations and 1 Court
                    Ruling Proving Voter Fraud Is Mostly
                    a Myth," *Washington Post*, July 9,
                    2014.

Investor's   "Voter Fraud Is Rampant, and
Business Daily   Democrats Ignore It," November 4,
                    2014. www.investors.com.

Howard Koplowitz	"Illegal Immigration 2015: Obama Executive Actions Could Result in Immigrants Voting, Voter Fraud, GOP Warns," *International Business Times*, February 13, 2015. www.ibtimes.com.
Suevon Lee	"Everything You've Ever Wanted to Know About Voter ID Laws," ProPublica, November 5, 2012. www.propublica.com.
Doug MacEachern	"Election Fraud Debate a Fraud," AZCentral, April 1, 2015. www.azcentral.com.
Bruce McConnell and Pamela Smith	"Hack the Vote: The Perils of the Online Ballot Box," *Wall Street Journal*, May 28, 2014.
Leon Neyfakh	"Why Can't Ex-Cons Vote?," *Slate*, March 17, 2015. www.slate.com.
Heather Digby Parton	"GOP's Maniacal New Vote Scheme: What Wingnuts Are Hatching to Keep the 'Riff-Raff' Away," *Salon*, October 23, 2014. www.salon.com.
Mark Pomerleau	"Online Voting Still Faces Security Issues," GCN, March 25, 2015. www.gcn.com.
Robert D. Popper	"The Voter Suppression Myth Takes Another Hit," *Wall Street Journal*, December 28, 2014.

Jamin B. Raskin — "Legal Aliens, Local Citizens: The Historical Constitutional and Theoretical Meanings of Alien Suffrage," *University of Pennsylvania Law Review*, Vol. 141, 1993. http://scholarship.law.upenn.edu.

Thomas Sowell — "Voter Fraud and Voter ID," RealClearPolitics, November 4, 2014. www.realclearpolitics.com.

David Talbot — "Why You Can't Vote Online," *MIT Technology Review*, November 5, 2012. www.technologyreview.com.

Sam Wang — "The Great Gerrymander of 2012," *New York Times*, February 2, 2013.

Index